W9-BXG-713

The
Struggle for
Democracy in
Latin America

THE MACMILLAN COMPANY
NEW YORK · CHICAGO
DALLAS · ATLANTA · SAN FRANCISCO
LONDON · MANILA
IN CANADA
BRETT-MACMILLAN LTD.
GALT, ONTARIO

THE
STRUGGLE FOR
DEMOCRACY IN
LATIN AMERICA

Charles O. Porter
and
Robert J. Alexander

New York
The Macmillan Company 1961

First Printing

The Macmillan Company, New York
Brett-Macmillan Ltd., Galt, Ontario

Printed in the United States of America

Library of Congress catalog card number: 61–5491

Dedicated to Frances R. Grant, who for three decades
has aided the struggle for democracy in Latin America.

CONTENTS

INTRODUCTION

Whose democracy? The U.S. brand?

Latin America is ready for democracy. Its people have fought bitter battles in recent years to prove this fact. However, the struggle to establish democratic government on a firm basis still goes on.

We feel that this struggle deserves the support of the people of the United States. It is to the discredit of the citizens and government of this country that all too frequently in recent years the power and prestige of the United States have been thrown into the balance on the side of the dictatorships. This has contributed to today's major crisis in relations between the United States and Latin America.

If good relations are again to be established between the two Americas, the people of the United States must be made aware of the facts concerning the struggle for democracy in Latin America. In the pages that follow we have attempted to present both the historical roots of this battle and some of the recent incidents in it. We hope that it will make at least a small contribution toward the "agonizing reappraisal" of United States

Western Hemisphere policy, which began with the ill fated visit of Vice President Richard Nixon to South America in May, 1958.

Definition of Democracy

Latin American democrats mean the same thing by "democracy" that we do. However, since the word has been so much misused and abused in recent years, it may be worth while to define what it is that we *do* mean by it.

Democracy, as we understand it, consists basically of two things: the right of the majority of the adult population to choose their leaders; and the right of the minority to continue to function legally, to attempt to become the majority.

There are two corollaries to these fundamental constituents of democracy: free and honest elections; and individual freedom. Individual freedom means the right to think, to speak, to print, and to organize.

This definition of democracy is perhaps a standard one. However, it merits restatement. This is the faith which most politically literate Latin Americans profess, just as it is the creed in which every United States citizen is presumed to believe.

Attempts to Discredit Latin American Democracy

It is not unusual for North American journalists, and even for so-called "experts" in Latin American affairs, to adopt a cynical attitude toward democracy in the countries below the Rio Grande. They tend to regard all political struggles in Latin America as mere contests between "ins" and "outs," between a dictator and someone else aspiring to be a dictator. All politics in the area, according to those who hold this view, is "personalist," a conflict among individual ambitious leaders, with little real meaning or ideological content.

According to many North Americans, the people of Latin America have no real conception of what democracy is all about.

They cite the prevalence of dictatorship over long periods in most of the Latin American nations, and the frequent failures of attempts to establish democratic régimes. They note the widespread illiteracy in the region, the supposed "lack of a middle class," and other social conditions which act as a brake on the development of democracy. All of these facts, they say, are "proof" that democracy is impossible in these countries.

This same line of argument is frequently used by the dictators and their apologists, who seek to picture such tyrannies as "inevitable" or even as "benign." In Peru, Venezuela, and some other nations which have been frequently subjected to dictatorial régimes, a school of sociological thought has developed around the fundamental proposition that the people of these countries are "unprepared" for democracy, and that they are, therefore, better off under a dictator.

Forces Favoring Democracy

Two fundamental facts are overlooked in this argument. First of all, it does not take into account the economic and social changes in Latin America which have been paving the way for political democracy. In the second place, this argument ignores the fact that a dictatorship is a poor school in which to learn how to practice democracy. The best way to learn how to conduct a democratic government is to attempt to conduct one.

As we shall see in a later chapter, it is no longer true that there is no middle class in Latin America. Nor is illiteracy any longer the great handicap that it was once considered to be. There have been numerous experiments in Latin America which indicate that lack of ability to read and write need not be an insurmountable obstacle to intelligent participation in the process of self-government.

The development of middle classes has led to the growth of political parties with meaningful programs and philosophies. They represent the interests of various groups in the community, rather than those of any particular *caudillo* or leader. Although the personal influence of individual leaders is still of importance in these parties—as it is in those of all democratic countries—the parties are continuing organizations with an active life between elections, and are not merely temporary vehicles for placing one particular leader in power. Thus, although personalism in politics is by no means completely dead, it is certainly of declining importance and is no longer a serious impediment to the development of political democracy in many of the Latin American countries.

These new political parties have a long tradition of democratic aspirations on their side. It is notable that the constitutions of Latin America have almost without exception been democratic documents, even though they have often been twisted, violated, or ignored by dictators. There is little doubt that the Latin American ideal of government for more than a century and a half has been that of political democracy. The early constitutions were generally copied from those of the United States or France, or, in some cases, that of Great Britain. In more recent decades the constitutions have generally tended to acquire a more distinctly native tone, but they have, for the most part, remained democratic documents.

The dictators themselves have long paid homage to this democratic tradition in Latin America. Even the most tyrannical and brutal among them has felt called upon periodically to submit to "reelection," in spite of the fact that the reelection period was frequently one in which the stresses and strains of the dictatorship have been sharpest. One of the reasons for the fall of Venezuelan dictator Marcos Pérez Jiménez in January, 1958, was the fact that he had violated this unwritten law of reelection. Instead of going through the forms of reelection, he had substituted a "plebiscite" in which the voters had only him to vote for. Even a rigged election would have been preferable to this Napoleonic and Hitlerian innovation.

Also indicative of the democratic traditions in Latin America is the fact that few régimes of a totalitarian ideology have come to power in the area. The Vargas dictatorship from 1937 to 1945 and perhaps the Perón régime in Argentina were two of the few exceptions to this. Even they did not go anywhere nearly as far as the European totalitarians in denigrating and condemning democracy.

Finally, the most convincing evidence of all of the desire for democracy in Latin America has been the valiant fight which people of various of the Latin American countries have waged against dictatorships, particularly since World War II. In spite of the most bitter persecution, heroic groups of professional people, students, workers, and others have fought against the dictatorships of Odría in Peru, Perón in Argentina, Pérez Jiménez in Venezuela, Rojas Pinilla in Colombia, Batista in Cuba, Stroessner in Paraguay, and even have carried on the apparently forlorn struggle against the nearly thirty-year-old tyranny of Trujillo in the Dominican Republic.

Extent of Democracy and Dictatorship in Latin America

This string of names of tyrants is evidence that the fight for democracy has by no means been won. Although most of the dictatorships which these men presided over are now a thing of the past, the democracies that have replaced them are still uncertainly in power; the danger of a return to tyranny has not been eliminated. The struggle for democracy goes on.

Certainly there are few countries in Latin America which as yet have thoroughgoing democratic régimes, but this is not a unique problem. There are few countries anywhere in the world that are truly democratic. However, as this is being written (June, 1960), most of the nations of Latin America are either under democratic rule or are evolving in that direction.

A few of the Latin American nations have a proud heritage of political freedom and democratic government. Chile has had but one dictatorship in the twentieth century, and has successfully evolved from an aristocratic, oligarchic democracy into one in which the masses play the leading role. It has come thus far with a minimum of upheaval and confusion. Uruguay has had a democratic government throughout the twentieth century, with the exception of a mild régime of force during the middle 1930's, of which the Uruguayans are duly ashamed. Costa Rica also has a long history of democracy, interrupted only by short-lived strong-arm dictatorships during World War I and the middle 1940's.

In most of the other nations of the region democratic administrations have been more sporadic, less established, or of more recent vintage. In some there is wide freedom of speech, press, and assembly, but elections are so managed that the opposition has little chance to win. In some others, the evolution toward democracy is seriously handicapped by the continuance of a tradition of changing governments by force, and slowness on the part of political groups to adapt themselves to a process of constitutional change. In still others, there is freedom for the individual, and elections are honest, but political activity is still limited to a very small fraction of the population.

In a few unfortunate countries—the Dominican Republic, Paraguay, Haiti, and Nicaragua—democracy has not yet triumphed. These nations are still ruled by petty tyrants who are able to make a mockery of their countries' constitutions and rule only because they have the armed force to keep themselves in power.

In several of the countries which have just recently thrown off dictatorships, the fate of democracy is still in the balance. Although a tyrant has been overthrown, there are still powerful and ambitious men who would like to see another one installed. In these nations the democratic elements need all the self-sacrifice and vision they can muster, and all the help and sympathy from outside that can be made available to them. The greatest disappointment has been Fidel Castro of Cuba. He promised his followers free elections and individual freedoms. Instead he has established a pro-Communist dictatorship in Cuba, a tragic perversion of the high hopes which his victory over Batista aroused throughout the hemisphere.

Many North Americans are unhappy and even skeptical about the limited degree to which democratic tenets have as yet been applied in some of the nations which are struggling toward the achievement of a civil and constitutional government, subject to the will of the people as expressed at the polls, and vigilant in protecting the rights of the individual. To these fellow citizens we need only point out that the process of making democracy work is a long and tedious one, which the people of the United States themselves have not as yet completely mastered, as the incidents at Little Rock and the meteoric success of the late Senator Joseph McCarthy bear ample witness. If the Latin American democrats are to succeed, they need the understanding and the encouragement of their fellow Americans to the North.

Responsibility of the United States

Whether it likes it or not, the United States has great influence in the struggle between democracy and dictatorship in Latin America. Almost anything the United States government does or does not do has repercussions in Latin America. Even the attitudes of influential newspapers in this country are closely watched in the other republics of the hemisphere, as are statements about Latin American affairs by leading figures in United States public life.

It is important that the United States use wisely the leadership and influence in the Western Hemisphere which has been thrust upon it. The first essential for such wise use of influence is to be well informed.

The government of the United States should use all the weight of its prestige and power to advance democracy in the neighboring countries to the South. This does not mean that the United States should overtly intervene in the internal affairs of the Latin American nations. Certainly, democracy is not something that can be imposed from without. However, it does mean that the United States should never lose an opportunity to show its fraternal solidarity with those countries which possess democratic régimes, and its sympathy for those who are struggling against tyranny in the countries still dominated by dictatorships. It means that the United States should never again make the mistake which it has made so often in the recent past of going out of its way to praise and flatter dictators and to extend economic and military help to their governments.

The United States can also help the development of a sound democratic atmosphere in the Latin American countries by a wide-gauge program of economic cooperation. Dictatorships and totalitarian movements are bred by economic crisis and discontent.

Conclusion

In the chapters that follow we shall trace the historical background of the struggle for democracy in Latin America, and sketch the changes which have recently strengthened the democratic forces in this struggle. We shall then trace those forces which are working in favor of democracy and those which are hindering its development. We shall take note of some of the more recent battles in the continuing war between democratic and dictatorial tendencies in the region. Finally, we shall outline in more detail the role which we feel that the United States should play in the struggle for democracy in Latin America.

CHAPTER ONE

HISTORICAL
DEVELOPMENT OF
DEMOCRACY

The people of the Latin American countries had little practical experience with democracy during the colonial period. There did not exist in the Spanish, Portuguese, and French colonies any institutions comparable to the colonial legislatures which characterized the English dependencies along the eastern fringe of North America. The power of the purse, control over the military, and general administration remained firmly in the hands of officials appointed by the governments of the "mother countries."

There were numerous reasons for this contrast between colonial Latin America and the English-speaking colonies. One of these was the difference between the areas conquered by Spain and those acquired by the English. The Spaniards found relatively highly developed Indian civilizations in many of the regions they colonized. Mexico and much of Central America as well as the whole area from southern Colombia to Bolivia in South America were regions already organized into more or less efficient empires. The populations were large. The people were sedentary, accustomed to agriculture, and, sometimes, to mining.

After a relatively easy conquest of these Indian empires, the Spaniards were able to graft themselves onto an existing social structure and to exploit it to the full. The Spaniards also found quantities of precious metals, which they could force the Indians to mine for them. Those Spaniards who were not engaged in mining were able to get vast grants of land—with the Indians resident on them—and to force the Indians to cultivate the land and supply the Spanish landlords with a substantial income.

The situation in Portuguese America was not too dissimilar from that in the Spanish colonies. In Brazil, the Portuguese early found products—Brazil nuts and diamonds, for example—which could be gathered and mined by natives or by imported Africans and sold for the benefit of the Portuguese. They were also able to develop in northeastern Brazil a patriarchal sugar plantation society, based upon African slave labor and exploitative of both human beings and the land. The Portuguese colonies, like the Spanish, were thus largely based on the exploitation of natural resources through the indigenous or imported servile laborers.

This situation deeply influenced the mother countries' attitude toward their colonies. Spain, Portugal, and France never forgot for one moment that the purpose of the colonies was to provide wealth for the home country. The gold and silver, and the wealth from sugar, diamonds, Brazil nuts, and other products were channeled into the Iberian Peninsula and went far toward explaining the dominance of this area—and particularly of Spain —over European politics during the sixteenth century, "the Century of Gold," as the Spaniards still call it.

The situation in the English colonies was entirely different. It soon became clear that there was little if any precious metal to be found along the heavily wooded coasts of North Atlantic America. Furthermore, the indigenous population was still in a savage or semisavage state, depending as much on migratory hunting and fishing as upon agriculture. The Indians of eastern North America, unlike those further to the south, were unwilling to submit to forced labor on behalf of the invading white man. They fought bloody wars to preserve their hunting grounds. Sometimes they fought until they were practically annihilated; and sometimes they retreated farther into the interior.

The upshot of this situation was that those who came to the English-speaking colonies were not able to impose themselves upon an already going society and exploit a large indigenous population. The English colonists had to work if they were to eat. Hence, the great majority of the early settlers became farmers or mechanics or tradesmen.

The fact that there was not easily available wealth to be exploited in the English colonies influenced the attitude of the English government toward these far-off outposts of empire. For almost a century and a half the English authorities paid relatively little attention to the colonies. Since, with the exception of tobacco, and to some degree indigo and rice, these provinces were bringing in little of value to the English economy, the English government did not seek to exercise very strict control over their affairs. Furthermore, throughout the seventeenth century and the first half of the eighteenth, the English were so embroiled in European rivalries and wars, that they had little time to pay attention to their rather unproductive colonies.

Undoubtedly, the different political institutions in the Iberian countries and in England help to explain the different governmental organizations in their respective colonies. In England, the power of Parliament, which had been expanding slowly since its establishment during the Middle Ages, grew rapidly during the seventeenth century, the period during which colonization got under way in North America. The Civil War of the middle of the century and the "Glorious Revolution of 1688" which deposed James II firmly established the superiority of Parliament over the monarch. Parliament's power continued to expand during the eighteenth century.

It was logical, therefore, that little parliaments should develop in that part of the English realm which lay across the Atlantic. The colonial legislatures were merely replicas in America of the older body at home. They exercised the same kind of control over the purse and generally had the same attitude of caution and reserve with regard to the Crown-appointed colonial governors as did Parliament toward the king back home.

In Spain, on the other hand, the battle between Parliament and the Crown was won early in the sixteenth century by the king. Charles V, soon after taking the throne, defeated the last attempt of the parliamentarians to defend their rights. The influx of gold and silver from America made it unnecessary for the king to go to Parliament for funds—as he had to do in Britain—and absolutism became dominant not only in Spain itself, but in the colonies. Much the same thing was true in Portugal.

Furthermore, the power of the Spanish sovereign was reinforced by the absolutism of the Spanish Church. The Reformation never really got started in Spain, and the terrible weapon of the Inquisition was used to uproot any religious dissidence. Although it was not as powerful in America as in Spain itself, the Inquisition undoubtedly did much to reinforce the religious uniformity which characterized Spanish America.

In English America religious heterodoxy became general. The seventeenth century was the era of great religious disturbance in Britain, and the right to dissent from the Established Church was finally recognized, first for Protestants, and later for Catholics. Hence, English America had its Calvinist and its Catholic colonies as well as its Anglican ones. Religious differences forced a certain degree of tolerance and compromise in English America, and tolerance and compromise are integral parts of political democracy.

Throughout the colonial period the governments of the Spanish, Portuguese, and French empires in America were in the hands of officials appointed from Europe. In the case of Spanish America, there were six viceroyalties at the end of the colonial period, those of Nueva España (Mexico), Nueva Granada (Col-

ombia, Venezuela, and Ecuador), Peru, Chile, the Rio de la
Plata, and Santo Domingo. Under the viceroys there were captains general in the various provinces. None of these officials was
checked by a locally elected legislature. However, in order to
be sure that the viceroys did not abuse their vast powers and
attempt to establish themselves as independent monarchs, the
Spanish Crown maintained a complicated series of checks and
balances of its own. These included Audiencias, semijudicial
bodies which investigated the activities of the viceroys and other
subordinate officials and administered the viceroyalties ad interim
between viceroys. They included also special investigators who
were sent from time to time to check on the accounts and
administration of the officials appointed by the Crown. In addition to all these, the high officials of the Church, also appointed
from Spain, undoubtedly served as counterbalances to the power
of the viceroys and other officials.

In all this there was no room for popular representation. Nor
was there much room for participation even by Spaniards born
in the New World, the so-called "Creoles." This, indeed, was one
of the principal grievances which led to the movement for independence in the early years of the nineteenth century.

The situation was not basically different in the Portuguese
colony. A viceroy appointed from Lisbon directed the affairs of
the Brazilian part of the empire. When the King of Portugal
moved to Brazil in 1808 in the wake of the Napoleonic invasion
of his homeland, he brought with him a large retinue from the
Portuguese court, whose arrogance and monopoly of all positions
of importance in the government went far to convince the
Brazilians of the need for independence.

Effect of the Wars of Independence

The wars of independence during the first quarter of the
nineteenth century did little to bring about more democratic
governments. Although the revolt against Spain began in some

cases as an uprising of the masses, or at least of the urban middle classes, by the end of the independence movement the net effect had been to pass power from the hands of officials appointed from Spain to those of members of the American-born aristocracy and landed oligarchy. Thus, in Mexico a movement which, under the leadership of Fathers Hidalgo and Morelos, began as a revolt of the Indian peons, ended up in 1821 under the leadership of a large landholder, Agustín de Iturbide, who declared himself Emperor Agustín the First.

The independence movement was led by intellectuals, mainly young men of the American-born aristocracy, who were much influenced by the ideals and ideas of the Enlightenment and the American and French Revolutions, and by elements of the group which was economically dominant in the colonies, the landlords. The latter resented the Spanish domination of the administration, but certainly wanted the revolt to go no further than the mere transfer of government power from Madrid-appointed officials to themselves. Although the masses were frequently mobilized to fight in the rebel armies, they were also not infrequently brought into the armies loyal to Spain, on the promise that the Crown would free them from the oppression of the local landholders. In no case, except Haiti, did independent spokesmen of the lower classes and the oppressed races—Indian and Negro—actually succeed in seizing control of the independence movement.

For the most part, the intellectual ideologues wrote the constitutions for the new republics of Latin America, while the landlord class, with the help of the Army and the Church, held the actual power. Thus, the constitutions, usually patterned on those of the United States or republican France, spoke glowingly of the rights of man and established the separation of powers and all the normal guarantees of democracy. In fact, these constitutions, with a few exceptions, were virtually dead letters.

Although the democratic constitutions of the Spanish American nations remained largely inoperative throughout the nineteenth century, they contained goals toward which the people could aspire. There were few rulers in the nineteenth century, and there have been few in the twentieth, who did not go through the forms of democracy. Although elections might be rigged and corrupted, they were generally held. Although the bills of rights were often ignored, they remained in the constitutions, and they could always be appealed to by those fighting a tyranny.

There are those who have professed to see only hypocrisy in this discrepancy between principle and practice in the Latin American countries. We do not believe that this is a correct interpretation. Rather it reflects a conflict between the enduring aspirations of the Latin American people and the ambitions of many of their rulers. The significant fact is that although individual tyrants may have been cynical and hypocritical in shrouding their oppression in democratic words, it was necessary for them to pay at least lip service to democracy as the price for remaining in power.

It was during the wars of independence that the armies began to play a major role in the politics of the Spanish American countries. The wars were generally long-drawn-out affairs, and were often devastating. When they were over, it was frequently the case that the only institutions protecting these countries from chaos were the army and the Church. The military leaders generally doubled as politicians. Brought up in the Spanish as opposed to the English tradition, the military leaders of Spanish American independence did not believe in civilian dominance over the military as did the military chiefs of the United States independence movement.

Generally, the Latin Americans were not so fortunate as to have a George Washington at the head of their revolutionary armies. Washington, in spite of all the hesitation, procrastination, and outright blocking of his efforts by the Continental Congress, never would accept the advice of some of his military colleagues to dissolve the civilian power. In Latin America, such was not the case. In any showdown between the military and the civilian authority, the military won.

Thus, by the end of the revolutionary movement against Spain, the Spanish American military men were used to intervening in political affairs. They have taken nearly a century and a half to get over this, and, as we shall see, have not as yet by any means completely accepted the idea of civilian domination of government.

The intervention of the military was looked upon with tolerance by the economically powerful groups in the new countries. The army represented stability and the defense of the new status quo. It was a block against attempts by lower-class elements to give the independence movement a social content. The military were defenders of the large landholding system and, at worst, the "generals" shared political power with the "doctors" coming from the aristocracy.

The Outcome of the Church-State Fight

The events of the latter half of the nineteenth century further solidified the position of the military as the ultimate arbiters in Latin American politics. The principal political issue of this period was the struggle over the powers of the Church. That mighty institution had come out of the colonial period as the largest landholder in many of the countries and a substantial one in most. It was immensely wealthy and engaged in many types of business. Its position was solidified in the constitutions of most of the nations, which proclaimed Roman Catholicism to be the state religion and, in some cases, the only legal one.

However, by the middle of the nineteenth century there was a growing feeling of resentment among laymen of the upper and middle classes against this predominant position of the Church. Liberal or anticlerical parties became arrayed against conservative or ultramontane groups in virtually all the republics. In some countries there were long-drawn-out struggles involving appeals to arms on both sides.

The net result of this struggle was to strengthen still further the position of the lay landholding group and of the army. In most countries the liberal groups won out and the Church was deprived to a greater or less degree of its rights and privileges. In a few cases Church and State were actually separated; in most the right of the Church to hold land and engage in business was severely restricted. The chief beneficiaries of these restrictions were landholding laymen, who were able to acquire for relatively little the lands and property which the Church was forced to give up.

With the weakening of the power of the Church, too, the importance of the armed forces rose. They generally participated in the victory of the liberals, and they loomed even larger than before as the defenders of the rights and privileges of the land-holding class.

In Brazil, the Church-State struggle contributed to the weakening and final overthrow of the empire. Brazil had been saved much of the turbulence of her Spanish-speaking neighbors because of the fact that Dom Pedro, the son of the Portuguese king, was the one to declare the nation's independence. He set himself up as Emperor Pedro I, and soon proclaimed a constitution which granted sizable powers to an elected Parliament. After a stormy ten-year rule, Dom Pedro I abdicated in favor of his son, Dom Pedro II, whose long rule of more than fifty years was marked by economic progress, civilian rule, and the outward trappings of a constitutional monarchy, though the country's economy continued to be based on Negro slavery.

The long war with Paraguay in the 1860's did much to strengthen the armed forces vis-à-vis the civilian power. Growing regionalism in the outlying parts of the empire, antislavery feeling —shared by the emperor himself—and a fight with the Church tended to undermine the position of the empire. Finally, the emancipation of the slaves by the emperor's daughter, Princess Isabel, acting as regent in the emperor's absence in Europe, was followed a few months later by a military *coup d'état* deposing the emperor and proclaiming a republic. The Brazilian army from then on remained a potent force in its country's politics.

Semifeudal Society of the Late Nineteenth Century

Fifty years after most of the Latin American countries had achieved their independence, these nations were still dominated by small oligarchies. The land, principal source of wealth and income, was held by a tiny group, largely descended from the European conquerors of three and a half centuries before. The great mass of the people, of mixed blood or of pure Indian or pure Negro stock, worked the land as sharecroppers, semiserfs or, in the case of Brazil, as slaves.

The landholding oligarchy, augmented by small mercantile classes in the cities and towns, not only monopolized the wealth, but possessed most of the education and virtually all the political power. The whole educational system was directed toward training members of the ruling élite and little or no attention was paid to the education of the masses of the people. Although politics was often bitter, degenerating not infrequently into military upheavals and even civil wars, the stakes in this game were all held by the landholding-commercial aristocracy.

The only other group which shared power with the economic oligarchy was the officer caste of the armed forces. By the last quarter of the nineteenth century the tradition of military intervention in politics was firmly established, and armed force was frequently used to settle the quarrels among the oligarchical politicians.

A spirit of nationality and of nationalism was almost non-existent. Most of the Latin American countries were, in fact, not yet unified nations. The lower economic and social groups had little feeling of loyalty to their "nations," and, indeed, were often ignorant of their very existence. The Indian still tended to be loyal to his tribe or linguistic group; the Negro's loyalty was still to his patriarchal master or to his racial group. The Europeanized upper classes felt that they had much more in common with the educated classes of the Old World than they did with the masses of people of their own nations.

In such a milieu democracy could not flourish. Throughout most of the first fifty or seventy-five years of independence, the majority of the Latin American countries were dominated by dictatorships of one kind or another. Some authoritarian régimes were frankly military dictatorships, others were "civil." To the masses of the people it made little difference, however, whether a "general" or a "doctor" occupied the presidential palace.

Even in those exceptional cases in which a degree of orderly, democratic procedure for changing governments had been established, only the members of the upper classes participated in it. Illiterates—the great majority of the population—were barred from the polls, and even where they were allowed to vote, they were generally marshaled to the polling booths and instructed in their voting by landlords or employers. This was the situation during most of the nineteenth century in Chile, for example.

Impact of European Industrialization on Latin America

During the last decades of the nineteenth century forces began to move in Latin America which were destined to transform the society and economy of these nations and to make their democratic constitutions more effective. These forces generally came from outside the area.

The industrialization of Western Europe and the United States during the nineteenth century made it increasingly necessary for these nations to look abroad for sources of raw materials, markets for their goods, and areas in which to invest their rapidly accumulating capital. One of the areas most affected by this process was Latin America.

Europeans and North Americans began to scour the Latin American countries for raw materials and foodstuffs. By the turn of the century, Argentina had become one of the globe's great breadbaskets, shipping vast quantities of grains and meat to the Old World. Chile's natural nitrates found a ready market; Brazil's coffee, the sugar of Cuba and Puerto Rico, the diversified minerals of Mexico and Peru, the cacao of Ecuador and Brazil, the wool and meat of Uruguay, all found increasingly receptive markets in Europe and North America.

This search for raw materials and foodstuffs stimulated the development of railroads and public utility services, which were needed to get them to market, and the development of banking and insurance agencies, which were required to finance and protect the new forms of economic activity.

Both the development of the new sources of mineral and agricultural products to satisfy the demands of the industrial countries and the establishment of the services to help get these products to market required large investments, which came from the same nations whose demands gave rise to the need for capital. British private investors, in particular, put their funds into the new railroads, electric power, and gas installations, banks, insurance companies, and even retail establishments. The Americans were not far behind by the turn of the century, and invested heavily in sugar, bananas, banking services, and, later, oil. The Germans, Italians, French, and other foreign investors also contributed to the building up of the capital equipment of the Latin American nations.

This process of "opening up" Latin America economically quickened the whole way of life of the region. The port cities, the centers from which the exports were shipped and into which imports were brought in repayment, began to grow rapidly. Important groups of wage earners employed under more or less modern conditions began to be brought together in the new mines, on the railroads, in the ports, in the construction industry. The artisan class grew to serve the increasing needs of the urban centers. The mercantile classes also found their businesses expanding by leaps and bounds, not only to serve the needs of the growing export-import trade, but to serve the people of the cities as well.

With the coming of the First World War an even more significant development occurred: manufacturing began on a significant scale. Cut off from their ordinary supply of imported consumers' goods from Europe and the United States, the Latin American countries began to produce these items for themselves. The textile industry, metal fabricating trades, food processing, and other manufacturing industries began to be of importance in the economies of the Latin American countries. The industrialization of Latin America can really be dated from the 1914-1918 period.

Growing Pressure for Democracy

With the growth of the middle class and the urban wage-earning working class, the dominant position of the landowning and mercantile oligarchy began to be challenged. New political parties began to appear which expressed the points of view and the aspirations of these new groups who demanded participation in government and resisted the role of the military in political affairs.

The new classes had interests in conflict with those of the old oligarchy. The new industrialists needed protection for their manufacturing establishments, and the rural aristocracy was opposed to this, both because it would make goods which they had to buy more expensive, and because they feared retaliation against their agricultural exports on the part of the industrial nations whose goods would be kept out by protective devices. At the same time, the new industrialist class wanted to see an expansion of the market for their goods, which meant that the rural peons, who had not received sufficient income to permit them to buy manufactured goods, had to be freed from their complete dependence on the landlords.

The industrial working class, too, had grievances against the rural oligarchy. The members of the group were drawn largely from the agricultural peon class, who naturally resented their old masters. Furthermore, they had the same interests as their new employers—the expansion of markets for manufactured goods and the protection of these markets from foreign competition. Finally, they sought and soon achieved extensive social and labor legislation, which inevitably had its repercussions on the workers of the countryside.

All these developments paved the way for making democracy something more than mere verbiage in the national constitutions. Not only did the new groups want to participate in the political life from which they had hitherto been shut out, but they also demanded freedom of organization, expression, and action.

These changes in domestic society and economy were reinforced by intellectual currents from abroad. With the growth of trade with the Old World, Latin America was no longer as isolated from general currents of world thought as it had been at an earlier period. Not only those members of the wealthy classes who could travel abroad or could afford to import books from Europe were influenced by ideas from Europe, but the middle and lower classes also began to be affected.

Even before World War I ideas of trade unionism and working-class political action had become popular among the artisans of the cities and such modern-type workers as those on the railroads, in the ports, and in the construction and printing industries. These ideas were spread both by the written word—books, newspapers, and other publications coming from Europe—and by the hundreds of thousands of immigrants who streamed into these countries from Europe. In the case of Mexico, Central America, and Cuba, the same ideas were spread from the United States.

The First World War, with its slogan of "making the world safe for democracy," and the Russian Revolution reinforced the growing feeling of revolt among the middle and urban working classes. In the 1930's the New Deal in the United States also had a profound impact on the thinking of these Latin American groups by demonstrating how a democratic government could be used to guide the economy, while leaving most of the means of production in private hands.

The growth of nationalism in the post-World War I period was partly a reflection of ideas prevalent in other areas of the world, but it was also the result of changes in Latin American society itself. The new middle and urban working classes, as active participants in public affairs, had a feeling of national identification which the rural peons had never enjoyed. Also, unlike the intellectuals of the old ruling group, they did not tend to identify themselves with their opposite numbers in Europe, but rather with the rank and file of their own countries. Though literate, these new groups were not primarily concerned with aping the manners and the fashions of the Old World, but rather with finding expression for the hopes and aspirations of the New World.

Nationalism was thus intimately connected with the desire for social, economic and political change. Nationalists sought to make their countries less dependent on the exportation of one or two products to the big industrial powers by building up local industries. At the same time, they sought to protect native workers against "exploitation" by the powerful foreign companies which controlled their nations' railways, public utility companies, mines, oil fields, and large agricultural enterprises. Finally, they attacked the old internationally-minded landholding aristocracy which had worked closely with the large foreign firms operating within their national frontiers.

Thus, by the middle of the twentieth century the picture of Latin America was fundamentally different from what it had been seventy-five years earlier. Economic transformation had brought into existence new classes which clamored for the right to participate in—and ultimately dominate—political life, while new ideas of social change and nationalism had reinforced the growing demand for more effective democracy.

CHAPTER TWO

FORCES FAVORING
DEMOCRACY IN
LATIN AMERICA

The contemporary struggle for democracy in Latin America is complex. There are supporters and opponents of the democratic process in all social classes and interest groups. However, in general terms, one can ascertain those elements in the society and civic life of the Latin American countries which are generally aligned on one side or the other of the struggle for democracy.

On the democratic side have been four principal groups: the democratic political parties, the trade unions, progressive middle-class elements, and a large segment of the intellectuals. Furthermore, in recent years there is considerable evidence that the Church is inclining more and more toward the side of democracy. We shall review the role of each of these groups in the democratic struggle in the twenty Latin republics of the hemisphere.

The Democratic Political Parties

Probably the most important groups working for the stabilization of the democratic way of life in Latin America are the political parties. These groups range widely in their ideologies and political philosophies, but there is a growing feeling of agreement among them that freedom is a basic prerequisite for their very existence. It is the political parties which have carried on the most tenacious battles against recent dictatorships.

It is common in the United States and Europe to discount and even make fun of the political parties of Latin America. They are said to be meaningless, mere vehicles of the personal ambitions of individual leaders. However, this attitude is a mistaken one. Those who continue to maintain it are indicating their ignorance of one of the most significant developments in Latin America during the twentieth century—the rise of ideological parties with more or less well defined doctrines and programs. Most of these parties are democratic in their orientation.

There are at least seven different types of democratic political parties in Latin America: the Conservatives, Liberals, Radicals, Socialists, Christian Democrats, Apristas or National Revolutionaries, and the peculiar *sui generis* party of the Mexican Revolution.

The Conservatives and Liberals

The Conservative and Liberal groupings are the oldest political organizations in Latin America, dating in many instances from the early days of the respective republics. Throughout most of the nineteenth century they dominated the political field. Generally speaking, the great issue which divided them was that of the relations between State and Church. The Conservatives were the great supporters of the entrenched position of the Catholic Church in the legal structure, economy, and social system of the Latin American countries. The Liberals, on the other hand, were anticlericals. By the end of World War I the Liberals had triumphed in most of the countries, with the result that the separation of Church and State had been achieved in several nations. Even in the rest, such civil functions as registration of births and deaths, administration of cemeteries, and control of education had passed from the Church to the State. At the same time, much of the vast property with which the Church had emerged from the colonial period had been stripped from it, and had passed either to the State or to individual laymen.

Although the struggles between the Liberal and Conservative parties were frequently violent and occasionally degenerated into civil wars, they normally involved only a very small fraction of the population. Politics was the monopoly of the select few who owned land or were engaged in urban trade. However, by World War I, political activity had begun to change, with the entry upon the scene of a sizable middle class and even working class in the cities. As a result, the Conservative and Liberal parties began to decline. They were able to survive only where they became the spokesmen for one group or another in the emerging social and economic struggle which came to dominate political life in most Latin American countries soon after the First World War.

Today there are still significant Conservative parties in Argentina, Chile, Colombia, Ecuador, Uruguay, Brazil, and Nicaragua. Generally, they represent the interests of the rural landowning classes, and get their electoral strength mainly from the ability of landowners to march their peons to the polls to vote as their masters instruct them. Exceptions to this generalization are found in Argentina, where since the fall of Perón, the traditional Conservative party has sought to adopt a "social" protective coloring in a vain hope of attracting some support from the followers of the ousted dictator; and Uruguay, where, although representing traditionally the interests of the rural landowner against those of the middle and working classes of Montevideo, the Partido Nacional (Conservative) has in recent years succeeded in gaining some support among the rural and urban wage earners, disillusioned in the long rule of the Colorado (Liberal) party.

There are Liberal parties of some consequence in Chile, Ecuador, Colombia, Honduras, Uruguay, Paraguay, and Nicaragua.

Generally, those Liberal parties have survived which have been able to become in some degree the spokesmen for the urban middle and wage-earning classes. This is the case in Ecuador, Colombia, Honduras, Uruguay, and Paraguay. An exception is Chile, where the Liberals are, if anything, more conservative than the Conservatives, and like them draw much of their support from agrarian landlords and their more or less obedient dependents. Another exception is Nicaragua, where the Liberal party became for two decades the tool of the Somoza dictatorship.

The Radicals

Three countries have had parties patterned more or less after the French Radical party: Argentina, Chile, and Ecuador. In each case they evolved out of the more advanced elements of the Liberal movement late in the nineteenth century. In Argentina, the Unión Cívica Radical usurped the Liberals' position as the spokesman for anticlericalism and for the urban and rural middle class. In Chile, the Radicals became the main representatives of the white-collar workers (a particularly potent political group in that country) and, most notably, the spokesmen for the government employees. In Ecuador, after a short period, the Radicals merged once again with the Liberals, who became the Partido Liberal Radical.

In Argentina the enactment of a democratic election law just before the outbreak of World War I led to a victory of the Unión Cívica Radical in the presidential election of 1916. For fourteen years thereafter, the Radicals presided over what was probably the most democratic period in Argentine history. They were ousted by a Conservative-army coup in September, 1930. Throughout the 1930's the Radicals remained the principal opposition to the overt and covert dictatorships of the period, undoubtedly representing a majority of the voters. With the advent of Perón, the Unión Cívica Radical became the principal rallying ground for the opposition to his dictatorship. They carried on a determined and valiant struggle with all the means at their command.

During the years of the Perón dictatorship, deep fissions developed within the Radical ranks. These came into the open after Perón's ouster. As a result, the Radicals split, in 1957, into the so-called Unión Cívica Radical Intransigente, headed by Dr. Arturo Frondizi, and the Unión Cívica Radical del Pueblo, led by Dr. Ricardo Balbin. These two men were the principal presidential candidates in February, 1958. Dr. Frondizi, the more extreme of the two in his campaigning and his denunciation of the established order, was the ultimate victor.

The Chilean Radical party was for three decades, from 1920 to approximately 1950, the principal bulwark of the Left. However, it frequently followed an opportunistic course, and was seldom unrepresented in the cabinet during this thirty-year period. From 1938 until 1952 the presidency was in the hands of three Radicals, Pedro Aguirre Cerda, Juan Antonio Rios, and Gabriel González Videla. By 1958 the party had lost considerable force, and its candidate in the presidential elections of that year came in fourth among six candidates, and last among the major nominees.

The Socialists

With the development of an urban wage-earning class late in the nineteenth century and the first decades of the present one, democratic Socialist parties began to develop in a number of the Latin American countries. In nations such as Brazil, Uruguay, Argentina, and Cuba, with relatively large European immigration, these parties tended to get the mass of their support from immigrants who had belonged to similar groups in their countries of origin. In other countries, such as Chile and Bolivia, the influence of Socialist literature from Europe and from Argentina strongly influenced the thinking of the founders of the Socialist parties.

There have been Socialist parties of some importance at one time or another in Argentina, Uruguay, Chile, Brazil, Panama,

Ecuador, Colombia, and Cuba. These parties have tended to suffer from two different kinds of weakness. On the one hand, some of them, such as those of Argentina, Uruguay, Cuba, and for many years that of Brazil, have tended to be too "European," with the result that after the passing of the immigrant generation, the Socialist parties tended to lose much of their influence. Other parties, such as those of Chile and Uruguay, have tended to be schizophrenic in their attitudes toward the Communists, with the result that they have from time to time been infiltrated and undermined by these totalitarians.

By the late 1950's the Socialists were a relatively small element among the democratic forces of the hemisphere. They constituted minor parties of some importance in Argentina, Uruguay, Chile, Peru, and Brazil. However, in none of these countries—with the possible exception of Chile—did they seem likely in the foreseeable future to become major forces in their countries' political life.

For the first time the Socialist International, with its headquarters in London, had taken a serious interest in the Latin American Socialists. Under the leadership of Humberto Maiztegui, a member of the Uruguayan Socialist party, the International established in 1956 the Latin American Secretariat, with headquarters in Montevideo. The parties officially associated with the Secretariat were the Argentine and Uruguayan ones, which belonged to the Socialist International, and the Chilean party, which did not. Maiztegui's principal objectives were to establish closer relations among the various Latin American Socialist groups, and between them and the Aprista or National Revolutionary parties.

The Christian Democrats

The Christian Democrats were of increasing importance by the late 1950's. Although one or two of these parties dated from before the Second World War, their increasing attraction to progressive-minded Catholics after 1945 was undoubtedly influenced by the success of similar parties in Europe after World War II.

By the late 1950's there were more or less important Christian Democratic parties in Argentina, Chile, Uruguay, Bolivia, Peru, Venezuela, and Guatemala. The oldest of these was the Unión Cívica of Uruguay, which for nearly forty years had shared with the Socialists and Communists those votes which did not go to the country's two major parties, the Partido Colorado and the Partido Nacional. Next in age and the most powerful of all the Christian Democratic groups was that of Chile. Established originally in the early 1930's by the Young Conservatives who withdrew from the Conservative party, under the name of the Falange Nacional, the Chilean Christian Democratic movement succeeded in gaining a considerable foothold in the labor movement, and was notable for the high caliber of its leadership. In 1957 the Falange Nacional merged with another dissident Conservative group of similar inclinations to form the Partido Democratico Cristiano. The PDC's candidate for the presidency in the 1958 election came in third, and the party had the second largest representation in Congress.

The other Christian Democratic parties were of more recent origin. That of Argentina emerged during the last days of the Perón régime and played some part in the overthrow of the dictatorship. It proved to be the fourth largest party in the country in the 1958 elections. Similarly, the Peruvian Christian Democrats emerged as an important force after the end of the dictatorship of General Odría in 1956. They were the country's second largest party, outstripped only by the Aprista party. Indeed, the Apristas showed considerable sympathy for the PDC, in spite of wide differences in program and philosophy, because they realized the need for the development of a rival party to the Partido Aprista which, though being anti-Aprista, would constitute a democratic opposition.

The Venezuelan party, the Partido Social Cristiano (Copei),

was established in 1946, and during the short democratic régime from 1945-1948, constituted the principal opposition to the dominant Democratic Action party. During the dictatorship which ruled Venezuela from November, 1948, until January, 1958, the Partido Social Cristiano was in the opposition, and after 1952 was the only party in the country which was not formally declared illegal, although it was prevented by the dictatorship from conducting any effective activity. With the overthrow of the Pérez Jiménez dictatorship, the Christian Socialists again emerged as an important political force, although relatively weaker than in the 1945-1948 period. The party's leader, Dr. Rafael Caldera, was elected President of the Chamber of Deputies early in 1959.

The Bolivian and Guatemalan Christian Democratic groups are of less importance. The former was established in the late 1940's and constituted part of the opposition both before and after the Revolution of 1952. The Guatemalan party emerged after the overthrow of the régime of President Jacobo Arbenz in 1954. It is by no means the country's largest party.

The Aprista or National Revolutionary Parties

All the parties which we have so far discussed have one thing in common: they are patterned after European models. Conservatives, Liberals, Radicals, Socialists, and Christian Democrats all are to be found in the countries of the Old World. The Aprista or National Revolutionary parties are in sharp contrast. They are organizations which have grown up in direct response to conditions in their respective countries and are in a true sense indigenous to Latin America. There has been no attempt to follow European models, and some of the parties of this type go out of their way to make it clear that they are peculiarly Latin American.

Although the very indigenous nature of these political organizations makes it more difficult to classify them (their programs are adapted to the situation in each individual nation), they do have certain general characteristics in common. First, they are multiclass parties, appealing to the urban working and middle classes, to the peasantry, and to the intellectuals in particular. Second, they are "revolutionary" in the sense that they seek fundamental changes in the traditional economic and social relations of their respective countries. They all favor advanced labor legislation, agrarian reform, the rapid extension of popular education, and the integration of oppressed racial and ethnological groups into the civic life of their respective countries.

In the third place, all these parties are nationalistic, particularly in economic matters. However, unlike some demagogic groups and individuals, and the Communists, they generally are not extreme in their nationalism. Fourth, they are all nonreligious parties. Some of them tend to be anticlerical, though generally they would prefer not to raise the religious issue at all. Finally, the Aprista* and National Revolutionary parties are democratic, seeking to establish the basis for a strong political democracy.

These parties are the single most important group of democratic parties in Latin America. They include the Partido Aprista of Peru, Acción Democrática of Venezuela, Liberación Nacional of Costa Rica, the Partido Febrerista of Paraguay, the Movimiento Nacionalista Revolucionario of Bolivia and the Partido Popular Democrático of Puerto Rico. They also include the exile parties Partido Revolucionario Dominicano and Vanguardia Revolucionaria Dominicana of the Dominican Republic, and at least two groups in Cuba: the Partido Auténtico and the Partido Ortodoxo. Finally, the Mouvement Ouvrier et Paysan of Haiti, led by ex-President Daniel Fignolé probably fits into this category.

The National Revolutionary parties of Peru, Venezuela, Costa Rica, Bolivia, and Puerto Rico are the largest political groups in their respective countries. The Paraguayan Febrerista Party is one

* The name derives from the initials of the Peruvian Alianza Popular Revolucionaria Americana (A.P.R.A.) founded by Victor Rául Haya de la Torre, and now known as the Partido Aprista Peruano.

of the three principal parties of that country, though it is difficult to know its actual rank among these since no real elections have been held in several decades. The two Dominican parties constitute the bulk of the exiled opponents of the Trujillo régime. All the Aprista or National Revolutionary parties recognize a kinship among themselves.

The Mexican Revolutionary Party

In a special category is the party which for over thirty years has led the Mexican Revolution and presided over the Mexican government. This group has had several names, including Partido Nacional Revolucionario, Partido de la Revolución Mexicana, and Partido Revolucionario Institucional (Institutional Revolutionary party—somewhat of a contradiction in terms), which it is now called. In some ways it is similar to the Aprista or National Revolutionary parties, but its long tenure in office, its peculiar structure and its bureaucratization give it special characteristics.

The program of this Mexican party is simple: the protection and continuation of the principles and program of the Mexican Revolution. In essence this means the defense of the agrarian reform, of trade unionism, of the secularization of the State and education, and of industrialization and economic development. The emphasis placed on various aspects of this program differs, depending upon who is President of the Republic, but the party's basic program remains much the same.

The organizational structure of the PRI is different from that of any other Latin American party. The PRI is a "collegiate" organization, that is to say, it has directly affiliated with it a considerable variety of other groups. Three so-called "blocs" make up the Partido Revolucionario Institucional. The Labor bloc consists of most of the principal trade union groups of the republic. The Agrarian bloc consists of the Confederación Nacional Campesina, which includes most of the peasants who have been the beneficiaries of the Revolution's agrarian reform. Finally, there is the so-called "popular bloc," consisting of numerous middle-class and professional organizations which support the Revolution.

The PRI has assured Mexico a high degree of political democracy, with a freedom of political expression and organization equaled in only a few other American countries. At the same time, the PRI has provided a vehicle for the expression of the points of view of many divergent groups. Through it they have been able to extend their influence on the government.

Summary of the Role of Democratic Parties

The rise of a wide range of political parties with more or less well defined ideologies and programs is highly significant and is one of the best guarantees of the future of democracy in Latin America. It has provided vehicles for the expression of the interests and the ideas of various groups in the population. It has provided the potential for a democratic alternation in power of different kinds of political organizations.

The growth of the political parties has helped to develop barriers against two of the principal evils of Latin American politics: militarism and personalism. Recent experiences have shown that the Latin American democratic political parties constitute organizations which are able to continue to exist and to resist all but the most violent persecution by military tyrants. Their members possess sufficient faith in their programs to be willing to continue to fight for them even though the parties are temporarily proscribed by a dictator, and the parties in many cases have sufficient organization and sufficient depth of leadership to make it possible to carry on sustained underground struggles against tyrannies.

It was the Radical and Socialist parties which carried on much of the continuing struggle against the Perón dictatorship; it was the political parties, and particularly Acción Democrática, which bore the brunt of the fight against the ten-year tyranny in Venezuela; it was the Aprista party which kept alight the fire of opposition to the Odría dictatorship between 1948 and 1956. In Cuba the Auténticos played an important role in the fight against the Batista régime. Similar situations have existed in other Latin American countries which have suffered from dictatorship during recent years.

Of course, it was not only the political parties who fought the dictatorships or overthrew the dictators. Particularly in the culmination of the struggle against the dictatorships, wide elements of the population who are outside of the party organizations have had a hand, and all or part of the military has almost always had a key role in the actual ousting of the various dictators. However, it cannot be denied that the continuing struggle, the day-to-day underground opposition, and the maintenance of agitation among various strata of the population have largely been the work of the democratic political parties.

Personalism, too, has diminished in importance with the rise of real popular political parties. Certainly the personalities of the leaders of the parties play a role in their success or failure, but the parties we have discussed are a great deal more than the personal vehicles of their founders and outstanding leaders. It is fair to say that none of the parties we have discussed would disappear from the scene or even be seriously diminished in importance because of the disappearance of the man who at the present moment happens to be its principal leader.

This is even true of the Partido Aprista of Peru, which more than most of the others has built its reputation and prestige on the personality of its founder, Victor Raúl Haya de la Torre. The ability of the party to reorganize and grow since 1956, in spite of Haya de la Torre's absence from the country during a good part of the time, is ample evidence of this.

Thus, as the political parties learn to put up a common front against attempts to establish new military dictatorships, and as politics becomes increasingly a contest among political parties committed to a democratic philosophy and competing among the voting population to obtain support for different programs and policies, the position of democracy in the Latin American countries is bound to become more solid and secure.

The Role of the Trade Unions

Although there are instances in recent Latin American history in which the trade unions have not been defenders of political democracy—cases in which they have come under the influence of one or another totalitarian group—generally speaking, the organized labor movement of Latin America constitutes a strong force on the side of democracy.

The trade unions are one expression of a group which has recently become an important force in the politics of the Latin American countries—the urban wage-earning class. The unions are eager to see the workers play a larger role in their countries' political life. They therefore seek to end the domination of politics by the agricultural landlords, the large urban merchants, and the military. They seek to use political activity as a means of bettering the economic and social lot of their members. In this sense, the labor movement is certainly on the side of greater political democracy.

In addition to this, the trade union leaders of Latin America are realizing more and more that in order for their organizations to function effectively, they must have an atmosphere of political freedom. Dictatorship inevitably means the suppression of the rights of the trade unions and of the workers generally. The majority of the trade unions of Latin America, therefore, are more or less closely associated with one or another of the democratic political groups which we have discussed. As such, they throw their weight behind the struggle for democracy in the hemisphere.

Perhaps the most significant thing about the role of the labor movement in this struggle is the fact that it presents for the first time a potential power center in opposition to the armed forces. The trade unions, by means of the strike, and particularly the general strike, are in a position to challenge the army's propensity to overthrow governments or impose governments by *coup d'état*.

There have been several cases in which this power has been demonstrated in recent years. One of the most striking occurred in October, 1945, when the Argentine army had temporarily ousted Juan Perón from power. Perón was restored as a result of a general strike and march on Buenos Aires by his labor supporters, and by the unwillingness of the armed forces to be responsible for the large amount of bloodshed which would have been necessary to impose its wishes on Perón's trade union backers.

Admittedly, this instance had mixed results insofar as democratic development was concerned. However, two incidents in Venezuela during 1958 were much more clearly prodemocratic in their effects. Discontented army elements twice attempted (in July and September, 1958) to overthrow the provisional government which had taken power after the fall of dictator Marcos Pérez Jiménez. Both these efforts were met by general strikes— *cum* lockouts—called by the labor movement and supported by the employers. A general strike supported by the Unión de Trabajadores de Colombia was to a considerable degree responsible for the overthrow of the dictatorship of General Rojas Pinilla in 1957.

There are indications that the leaders of the democratic parties are increasingly aware of the potentialities of the trade union movement as an ally in the struggle for democracy. There is no doubt that the democratic parties and the unions working together can go far toward curbing the habitual tendency of Latin American military men to oust the government of the day if they are for some reason unhappy with it.

The Position of the Progressive Middle Class

There are sizable groups among the middle class who are also supporters of political democracy in Latin America. The industrialist, mercantile, and professional groups associated with them generally have interests in conflict with the landowning and allied groups which monopolized political life until recent decades. Hence, these middle-class elements seek an extension of the base of political power, and tend to welcome the organized workers as allies. Although there are ultimately differences in interest between the industrial workers and their employers, at the present stage of things in most Latin American countries they have much in common, particularly in the face of the old oligarchy.

These same groups have reasons to be opposed to military dictatorships. Modern industry and the complicated economy to which it gives rise need the protection of law. The industrialists and their friends resent the arbitrariness of the military dictatorships; they resent the corruption and the favoritism which generally characterize this sort of government.

The industrialists are at least passively in favor of a democratic rather than a dictatorial régime. Although they may avoid overt opposition to a tyranny for fear of reprisal against their enterprises, they are certainly not likely to defend a dictatorship, and appear to be increasingly willing to help overthrow this type of administration or help to prevent it from coming to power in the first place.

It is notable that many Cuban industrialists contributed heavily to the coffers of the revolutionaries who were fighting the Batista dictatorship. It is notable, likewise, that a large segment of the Argentine industrialist class carried on a persistent fight against the Perón régime. After the overthrow of the Pérez Jiménez dictatorship in Venezuela early in 1958 the industrialists made it very clear that they favored the establishment of a democratic government and would use their influence as a class to prevent the return of a military dictatorship. In July and September, when elements of the army attempted coups against the provisional government, the industrialists supported the unions' general strike against the coups by a general lockout, which was of great importance in bringing about the failure of these attempts.

The Role of the Intellectuals

The Latin American intellectuals are by no means all supporters of political democracy. They have been penetrated by another element, by the Communist totalitarians, and each of the dictators of the area has found a certain number of time-servers among the intellectuals, willing to defend and justify their régimes. However, a great majority of the teachers, writers, artists, students, and other intellectuals are strong supporters of political democracy.

The leadership of the democratic political parties is generally drawn from the intelligentsia. Their knowledge of what is going on in other parts of the world, their social conscience, and their need for democracy as a guarantee of their own right of self-expression has put many intellectuals in the leadership of those political organizations which are fighting for a broadening of the base of political life and for the freedom necessary for the fullest development of the intellectual and spiritual capacity of the individual.

In many recent Latin American dictatorships the intellectuals have played very important roles as members of the opposition. Thus, it was the university students and faculty members who were the most militant opponents of Perón and who, along with the political parties, were the most consistent fighters against his dictatorship. The struggle of the Venezuelan students and professors against Pérez Jiménez brought about the closing down of the universities by the dictator on several occasions, and in the last months of the régime, the intellectuals formed a virtually solid front of opposition. The universities and their alumni among the professional people were among the most effective fighters against the Odría dictatorship in Peru. Finally, in the seven-year fight against the Batista tyranny in Cuba, the principal leadership came from the intellectuals, and particularly from the students. Thousands of students and young professional people joined the underground against Batista and many others joined the guerrilla forces fighting against him.

Perhaps one of the most important offshoots of the growing awareness among intellectuals of the importance of the democratic fight is the increasing militancy of the press of the hemisphere in its fight against dictatorial arbitrariness and abuse. Increasingly, the most important and influential newspapers of the various Latin American countries have come to regard an attack on one of them as an attack upon them all. The press has to a growing degree demanded freedom for itself, and tangentially has demanded all the other democratic freedoms as well. To a considerable degree this growing militancy of the press has been coordinated and reinforced by the Inter-American Press Association, which includes North American as well as Latin American publications.

A striking example of the attitude of many Latin American newspapers was the refusal of *El Tiempo,* dean of the Colombian press, to publish handouts of the censors during the Rojas Pinilla dictatorship. When *El Tiempo* was closed down as a result, newspapers throughout the hemisphere protested vigorously. Their campaign did not cease until the overthrow of Rojas Pinilla and the reappearance of *El Tiempo.*

This attitude of the press has been of particular importance in Latin America. The great newspapers of the region are outlets for the literary output of authors of the area, and for serious nonfiction writing as well, to a degree which is certainly not matched in North America. Furthermore, the insistence of the large journals with great prestige on freedom of the press is likely to benefit the smaller and more nonconformist periodicals as well.

The Position of the Church

The Roman Catholic Church in Latin America has not traditionally been on the side of democracy. Throughout the nineteenth century it seemed to be more preoccupied in many of these countries with protecting the property and privileges it had accumulated during the colonial period than in saving the souls of men. This struggle to defend its vested interests put it on the side of extreme conservatism and the defense of the *status quo*. Many of the dictatorships of the nineteenth and early twentieth centuries had the blessing of the Church.

However, since World War II, and particularly during the 1950's, there has been accumulating evidence that the Church in Latin America is undergoing a fundamental change of policy. Becoming aware of the profound changes which are in progress in the area, the hierarchy in various countries seems to have become convinced of the necessity of dissociating the Church from its traditional identification with economic conservatism and rule by force. Rather, the Church has inclined toward a kind of Christian Social policy in economic and sociological matters, and of tolerance for, if not outright support of, democracy in the political sphere. There are still countries in which this new policy is not as yet being applied, but the general tendency in Latin America seems clear.

It is notable that the Church played a very important role in the ousting of Perón in Argentina, of Rojas Pinilla in Colombia, and of Pérez Jiménez in Venezuela. It played a lesser but nonetheless significant part in the last year of the fight against the Batista tyranny in Cuba. Furthermore, the Paraguayan Church has brought considerable pressure to bear against the continuation of the Stroessner dictatorship in that country.

It is perhaps too early to say whether or not these individual actions of the Church hierarchy in various countries represent a fundamental change in policy throughout the area. However, if such is the case, the cause of democracy will have gained a recruit of very great importance, and of all the more importance because it has traditionally been aligned on the other side.

Summary and Conclusion

Thus, there are powerful elements working toward the stabilization of political democracy in Latin America. The two principal new class groups which have been brought into existence by the economic and social revolution of recent decades—the middle class and the urban working class—are generally favorable to the broadening of the base of political activity, to the establishment of orderly processes for changing government, and to the reinforcement of the fundamental freedoms. The majority of the intelligentsia of the area is similarly disposed. Finally, there are indications that one of the most powerful institutions of the old order, the Church, is undergoing a change of policy which is placing it, too, on the side of political democracy rather than oligarchic rule and dictatorship.

New institutions have developed which are capable of supporting political democracy. These include the workers' trade unions and the organizations of the industrialists and other middle-class groups. Most important of all, however, are the democratic political parties, which are carrying the principal burden of the day-to-day struggle to evolve a democratic political system. They have borne the brunt of the fight against the recent and still existing dictatorships, and their leaders perhaps understand most clearly the implications of the struggle for democracy.

CHAPTER THREE

FORCES OPPOSING
DEMOCRACY IN
LATIN AMERICA

The forces favoring democracy still must face powerful opponents. The forces opposing democracy can be divided into two types. First, there are institutions and interest groups which for their own reasons do not particularly care to see the evolution of a civilian form of government which rules as a result of the freely expressed will of the majority and guarantees to the individual the rights of freedom of speech, press, belief, organization, and action. Second, there are certain situations, generally hangovers from the past, which serve to hamper the development of modern democracy.

Those interest groups which are the chief stumbling blocks to democratic development are retrograde social and economic elements, a considerable part of the armed forces, certain ambitious politicians, and the totalitarian political parties. The principal remnants of the "old régime" which hamper the growth of democracy are illiteracy, a certain lack of appreciation even among many of those formally committed to political democracy of the full implications of a democratic system, and, finally, the power of antidemocratic tradition.

Retrograde Social and Economic Elements

The defenders of the old régime in Latin America have little concern for democracy, and, indeed, are frequently extremely hostile to the idea. This is particularly true of the semifeudal class of rural landlords, whose holdings are cultivated by workers —usually of a different race from the landholder—who are held in a greater or less degree of subjection and servitude. This element sees no virtue in changes that would give their tenants a voice in civic affairs, and would sooner or later destroy the landlords' privileged position. Associated with the rural landowner tend to be certain urban commercial interests which have been traditionally linked with the rural aristocracy.

These elements have carried on a bitter struggle against the democratic political parties, and particularly against those which have advocated a program of social and agrarian reform. In their eagerness to prevent the alteration of the *status quo*, these elements in such countries as Bolivia, Peru, Guatemala, and pre-revolutionary Mexico relied heavily on cooperation with the armed forces and supported dictatorships.

There is some indication in recent years that members of the oligarchy have been having second thoughts about the methods with which they have traditionally resisted social reform. This is particularly the case in Peru, where important persons of the oligarchy have come to the conclusion that change is inevitable, and that it is better that it come gradually and through the democratic process than by violent revolution, as in neighboring Bolivia. Furthermore, these same elements became increasingly impatient at the highhanded methods with which the army brass treated all civilians, including themselves. This part of the Peruvian oligarchy played a key role in putting an end to the latest of the long series of military dictatorships in that country—the régime of General Manuel Odría—in 1956.

The Role of the Military

The armed forces are probably the single most serious impediment to the development of democracy. There are perhaps only one or two countries in all Latin America in which the civilian politicians do not have to keep under active consideration what the military men's reaction is going to be to any measure which they undertake, and even the possibility that the armed forces will seek to oust the government, no matter how well entrenched in popular support that government may be.

In some countries the problem is greater than in others. There are a number of nations, such as Venezuela, Peru, Ecuador, and Paraguay, in which the army has dominated local politics almost without interruption since the achievement of national independence a century and a half ago. In these nations it is doubtful that the military will permit the evolution of a civilian, democratic régime under any circumstances.

The problem of the military is a complicated one. Its peculiar role as the arbiter of government and politics in many of the Latin American countries came about as the result of a combination of circumstances. The colonial civilians of Spanish and Portuguese America had little experience in self-government before the wars of independence. These same wars went on for a relatively long period of time and in some countries resulted in a great deal of devastation and destruction, as well as the creation of a serious power vacuum and a situation verging on chaos. Only the armed forces and the Church seemed to represent "stability" and "order." Furthermore, the economic and social élite found it necessary to depend heavily on the army to prevent the movement for national independence from becoming a profound social revolution. Finally, the army represented during much of the history of many of these countries one of the few ways through which young men of relatively humble origins could rise to positions of power, wealth, and influence.

Hence, the tradition of military intervention in politics became entrenched and powerful.

At the present time there are conflicting currents of thought and opinion among the military men themselves. There is undoubtedly a more or less strong element, even in the armed forces of those countries traditionally dominated by the military, which favors "the return of the soldiers to the barracks" and their dedication to their professional activities. Indeed, most Latin American soldiers will say, when asked, that this is the policy they should follow. However, there remains a strong element among the officer caste which gives only lip service to this attitude.

Another complicating factor at the present time is the growing importance of elements other than the army among the military. The navies and air forces of Latin America differ from the traditional military in several ways. First of all, they are much more highly trained and their work is much more technical, while at the same time they tend to devote more attention to their military duties and less to politics. The same is true of certain elements among the ground forces. These groups as a whole resent the domination of the armed forces by relatively uncouth and untrained soldiers of the old régime.

Finally, an important factor in the possible decline in the political influence of the military is the economic growth and diversification of the Latin American countries. The development of industry and of a middle class provides avenues of advancement other than the armed forces for the ambitious young men of lower social strata. Hence, perhaps, the military will tend to attract in the future less the person who seeks a way to power and social prestige and more the person who is really attracted to military life as such.

In spite of the trends within the armed forces which we have noticed, the military remains a formidable barrier to the development of political democracy. It will be a long time before the soldiers completely give up the idea that they have a kind of divine right to interfere in political affairs to "save the country" or "clean up the mess," which they have in the past used as an excuse for their intervention. Militarism being the very antithesis of democracy, this penchant of the soldiers actively to engage in politics, using force as their ultimate argument, cannot help but be a retarding element in the struggle for democracy.

Ambitious Politicians

There are Latin American military men who argue that they are not entirely responsible for their intervention in politics; that ambitious civilian politicians are using them to further their own careers. There is more than a little truth in this.

It has been traditional in many of the Latin American countries for a politician who lost an election—whether honestly or through finagling—to turn to friends among the officers to help him seize power. There are still politicians in Latin America who are inclined to do this.

The rise of ideological political parties and the resulting decrease in the influence of personalism in Latin American politics are likely to decrease the importance of this tendency to appeal to the armed forces. Although the political parties are by no means completely unwilling to use the military to their advantage, they realize better than the personalist politician of old the dangers of armed forces intervention in political activity and the likelihood that such intervention will seriously hamstring the party and limit its freedom of action.

Nonetheless, the ambitious politician, unable to wait until he has won the support of his fellow citizens, remains a big stumbling block in the way of democratic development. At best, it will be a considerable time before this stumbling block has been removed.

The Totalitarian Political Parties

All the political parties which have arisen in Latin America in recent decades have not been democratic in their orientation. Latin America has had its share of totalitarian political organizations, some patterned after European models, such as the Fascists, Communists, and others of indigenous molds.

Several Latin American countries have had Fascist parties. The most important ones have been the Partido Nacista in Chile, the Partido Integralista of Brazil, and the Falange Socialista Boliviana of Bolivia. The first of these has passed out of existence, the second is now of minor importance, but the Falange is the second largest party and the principal factor in the opposition to the present government of Bolivia.

The Partido Nacista found its principal support among the people of German origin in the southern part of the Central Valley of Chile in the 1930's. For several years it made a great deal of commotion, organized groups of young storm troopers, who engaged in pitched street battles with political opponents in various Chilean cities. The Partido Nacista had some representation in the national congress, though it never became one of the country's major parties. Since World War II the party has disappeared, and its former leaders are to be found widely distributed among the numerous parties which characterize Chilean politics. As a group, the Nacistas are no longer a force of any importance in Chile.

The Partido Integralista also drew much of its support from partially integrated foreign communities in Brazil, particularly from German and Italian elements. It grew rapidly during the 1930's and by 1937 represented a major challenge to the government of President Getulio Vargas. However, when Vargas organized a *coup d'état* from the presidential palace in November, 1937, and established his own version of a Fascist corporate state, he simultaneously outlawed the Integralistas and deported their principal leader, Plinio Salgado, to Portugal. Subsequent to World War II, Salgado returned to Brazil and reorganized the Integralistas under the name of Partido de Representação Popular. However, it remained a small element in the Brazilian political picture—Salgado came in fourth among four contestants in the 1955 presidential election.

The Falange Socialista Boliviana was organized in the middle 1930's by a group of political exiles in Chile. It was frankly patterned after the Spanish Falange which became the only legal party in General Franco's Fascist régime. It remained a small party until the 1952 Revolution. Then the Falange Socialista Boliviana became the principal rallying ground for the right-wing opponents of the Bolivian National Revolution. Although the party leaders claim to have forsworn their previous loyalty to fascism, and to be "democrats," this is highly dubious.

The Communists

There is now a Communist party in every Latin American country. The Latin American Communists are like their counterparts in other parts of the world—their twin objectives are to support the Soviet Union in whatever policy it follows, and to establish a one-party dictatorship in their own particular country. They are part of the International Communist movement, and receive advice, instructions, and sometimes financial assistance from the international Communist apparatus.

The Communists' appeal in Latin America in recent years has been both social and nationalistic. They are very active in the trade unions, peasant organizations, and similar groups, and picture themselves as advocates of labor legislation, agrarian reform, and other social measures. At the same time, the Communists have been more nationalistic than the most rabid nationalists. They have known full well that the weight of Latin American nationalism was likely to be turned most strongly against the United States because of the preponderant position of the United

States in hemisphere affairs. They have therefore sought to stimulate nationalism as a means of dividing Latin America from the United States—and thus helping the Soviet Union in the Cold War.

From the beginning, the Communists have been the most frank apologists for the Soviet Union. Throughout the 1920's, 1930's, and 1940's they talked loudly about "the defense of the Soviet Union" as being their most sacred duty. Since World War II they have become somewhat more subtle, but during 1945 and 1946 the principal leaders of the Latin American Communist parties joined their opposite numbers in other parts of the world and announced publicly that if their countries were ever involved in war with the Soviet Union, the local Communist party would support the USSR and oppose the local war effort.

The Communists have had no difficulty in allying themselves with the Latin American dictators. At one time or another during the last couple of decades they have worked with the Benavides, Prado, and Odría dictatorships in Peru, with the Batista dictatorship in Cuba, with the régime of Somoza in Nicaragua, with Pérez Jiménez in Venezuela, with Perón in Argentina, with several antipopular administrations in Bolivia, with the Vargas corporate state dictatorship in Brazil, and with Trujillo in the Dominican Republic.

Since World War II the Communists have evolved a double-barreled technique to deal with the dictators. Their parties have been split in countries in which dictatorships existed, and one faction has supported the tyrant, the other has joined the opposition. This technique was applied in Perón's Argentina, Odría's Peru, Peréz Jiménez' Venezuela, and Batista's Cuba.

The Indigenous Totalitarians

In addition to the Communists and Fascists, which are both of European origin and inspiration, there have been some indigenous Latin American totalitarian parties during the last two decades. The most important of these have been the Partido Peronista of Argentina and Getulio Vargas's Partido Trabalhista in Brazil.

These parties have certain things in common. They were both organized from the government by their respective leaders, Juan Domingo Perón and Getulio Vargas. They both appealed principally to the urban wage earners, with a social program designed to win their loyalty, and succeeded in gaining the support of the majority of this group. Each put exaggerated emphasis on its leader's alleged role as "protector of the workers." Both were, in their inception at least, contemptuous of political democracy.

The Partido Peronista was outlawed in 1955 by the provisional government of General Pedro Aramburu, after the fall of the Argentine dictator. However, Perón continued to have the support of a sizable proportion of the country's wage earners, and the party was reorganized in 1959 under the name of Partido Justicialista. Many of those supporting it were no longer particularly anxious to see the deposed dictator return to power, but looked upon the movement which he had founded as the true party of the Argentine working class. This element would like to see the Partido Justicialista transformed into a democratic workers' party, but another sizable element still yearns for a return to the totalitarian dictatorship of the exiled general.

The Partido Trabalhista, too, went through a considerable transformation after the ouster of Getulio Vargas from power in 1945. It continued to be regarded as Vargas's party, and to enjoy the backing of the majority of the urban working class of Brazil. However, because Vargas himself decided to essay the role of a democrat during the late 1940's and early 1950's, the Partido Trabalhista became a democratic political party. After the suicide of Vargas in August, 1954, the party was sorely wracked by factionalism and plagued by opportunistic upstart politicians seeking to ride to office on the votes of the workers, but little concerned with the welfare of those who put them into government positions.

The Nature of the Totalitarian Threat

The Vargas and Perón parties were examples of what might be called the Jacobin Left. Since January, 1959, the outstanding representative of this trend of Latin American political sentiment has been Fidel Castro.

These Jacobins, like their predecessors of the French Revolution, are nationalistic to the point of xenophobia. They seek a fundamental revolution at whatever cost, with little regard for whether this upheaval results in political democracy. Indeed, democracy appears to them too slow for their purposes. They are inclined to see it as a deception for the benefit of the exploiters. They tend to look upon the Communists as their allies.

Since the victory of Castro, the Jacobins have grown in influence throughout Latin America. A number of dispersed parties and groups have gravitated toward the erratic Cuban leader. He has fostered the split of the restless elements from the parties of the democratic Left. The Jacobins have thus become a major factor in the Latin American political scene.

The totalitarians represent a serious potential threat to democracy in Latin America. However, this threat does not seem to most Latin Americans to be as pressing as that of indigenous military dictatorships which have plagued their region since World War II. The totalitarians, including the Communists, are a future menace rather than an immediate threat to democratic development in most Latin American countries.

The totalitarian threat to democracy is qualitatively different from that coming from other groups which we have discussed. Unlike the rural landlords and their allies, or the military, or most of the ambitious politicians, the totalitarians are able to arouse a good deal of popular support. They make an appeal to the urban working and middle classes and even to the peasantry which is in many ways like that of the democratic political parties of the moderate Left, an appeal which in many ways conforms to the interests of these classes. The totalitarians promise social legislation and agrarian reform, and play on the nationalistic sentiments of the masses. At the same time they argue that social reform, economic development, and the defense of national sovereignty cannot be achieved by democratic methods. They try to discredit the checks and balances of democracy as "bourgeois" or "plutocratic" nonsense designed to defend the *status quo.*

This kind of appeal is potentially very dangerous. Perón demonstrated its potency when he promised—and delivered to a considerable degree—a wide range of reform in exchange for the workers' freedom. The Communists' appeal is very similar, although they are usually not quite so frank in their approach as the Argentine dictator was.

The problem of the totalitarians can best be met in the long run by the parties of the democratic Left—the Socialists, Radicals, Liberals, Christian Democrats, and most of all by the indigenous Aprista or National Revolutionary parties. These groups make their appeal to the same strata toward which the totalitarians look for support. They are sincere advocates of programs of labor legislation, agrarian reform, industrialization, and political democracy which the totalitarians use in varying degrees for propaganda purposes but have little intention of putting into effect if they should chance to come to power.

The success of the democratic Left and the totalitarians is likely to vary inversely. If the democratic parties are successful in carrying out wide programs of social reform, are able to push forward with reasonable rapidity the economic development of their nations, so as to give hope of rising levels of living, and if they are able to create a stronger basis for the national sovereignty of their respective nations, they will cut the feet out from under the totalitarians of all stripes. To the degree that the democratic Left fails in this endeavor, the totalitarians are likely to be the chief gainers.

The Problem of Illiteracy

Certain conditions which survive from the preindustrial period are hampering the struggles for democracy in Latin America. One of the most important of these is widespread illiteracy. The proportion of illiterates in the population varies widely, from 15-20 per cent in Uruguay and Argentina to 95 per cent in Haiti.

The illiteracy of the Latin American rural masses makes them easier victims of exploiting landlords and merchants. At the same time, it serves to keep the peasants ignorant of their rights as citizens. A great gulf exists between the literate rulers and the illiterate ruled. In the cities, illiteracy hinders the incorporation of workers into the new industrial economy and hampers their active participation in politics.

The inability of large parts of the citizenry to read and write is a drawback to the development of democratic political parties. Illiteracy breeds parochialism and a lack of awareness of important national issues. Not infrequently it even results in the illiterates being unaware of their membership in the nation.

The illiterates are accustomed to give their loyalty to individual employers and landlords, and they transfer this custom to public life, thus strengthening the personalist tradition in Latin American politics. Because of their inability to read and their unfamiliarity with political ideas and ideologies, it is more difficult than it might otherwise be to appeal to them in more or less sophisticated terms and to educate them on great national problems.

Lack of Appreciation of Implications of Democracy

There are those in both parts of the hemisphere who argue that Latin America is still far from the achievement of democracy because the people of the area do not really know what the concept means. Although those who argue thus greatly exaggerate their case, there is a kernel of truth in it.

One of the most difficult things for Latin Americans to learn has been that it is possible honestly to lose an election. It is hard for many to conceive that their opponents actually may be able to win the support of a majority of the voters without any recourse to corruption, violence, or other undemocratic means.

Allied to this is the tendency of some who believe themselves democrats to interpret any opposition as subversion. Not infrequently, even mild criticism is regarded as an attempt illegally to oust the régime in power. In some cases there is a certain justification for their outlook by the group in power, because there is still some tendency, even among democratic elements in Latin America, when they are in the opposition, to obscure the fine but all-important line between criticism, even violent criticism, and attempts to overthrow the incumbent administration by recourse to force.

One cannot deny that these problems exist. However, one cannot deny either that there is an increasing number of instances in recent years in Latin America in which the democratic game has been played loyally and in which the opposition has been allowed to win and to take office. This occurred in the 1946, 1952, and 1958 presidential elections in Chile, in the 1958 election in Uruguay, in the 1952, 1956 and 1960 elections in Ecuador, in the 1958 election in Costa Rica, in the 1950, 1955 and 1960 elections in Brazil, and in several other instances.

The Latin American democratic political leaders are a good deal more sophisticated than they are believed to be by many North American observers, and even many Latin Americans. Most of the leaders of the democratic political parties are well aware of the need for a healthy opposition in a democracy, they are quite conscious of the necessity for honest and uncoerced elections, they are convinced that when the opposition wins it must be allowed to take power. Although it is still necessary to be on guard against the old tendencies, they are by no means any longer the rule.

The Power of Tradition

One final stumbling block in the way of the development of healthy democracy in Latin America must be mentioned. This is the power of the antidemocratic tradition. Although the Latin Americans generally have aspired to democracy since the wars of independence, in practice democracy was until recent decades largely conspicuous by its absence. The force of this past history still weighs on contemporary politics.

This is probably particularly significant with regard to the role of the armed forces. The most important factor on the side of continuing military meddling in politics is the power of tradition. The generals and colonels are used to throwing their weight around and to making and unmaking governments at will. It is hard to break this tradition. It takes education, a high degree of understanding of the role of the armed forces in a modern democratic state, and much forbearance on the part of individual military leaders for this tradition to be overcome.

However, the antidemocratic tradition is not confined to the leaders of the armed forces. Civilians, too, in many countries have thought the normal method of ousting the régime in power to be that of the barracks revolt and the *coup d'état*. They too must come fully to realize that one of the burdens of democracy is getting along with a régime one does not like until the next polling day, when one can attempt to convince the voters that one's dislike is justified and that they should do something about it. The tradition of conspiracy and *coup d'état* must be broken among the civilian politicians as well as among the military men.

Summary and Conclusion

Although there are still formidable barriers in the way of a smooth development of political democracy in Latin America, these barriers are being overcome. Although one should not underestimate their importance, neither should one exaggerate them and come to the conclusion that democracy is impossible. Perhaps a fuller awareness of just what the principal hazards to democratic development are is one of the greatest needs both for the Latin Americans who are trying to hasten this development and for the North Americans who are trying to understand it.

CHAPTER FOUR

THE STRUGGLE
FOR DEMOCRACY SINCE
WORLD WAR I

The struggle for democracy has become a dominant issue in Latin American affairs since World War I. Before that time politics in the area was at best confined to a small ruling group which seldom sought to bring into civic life the great masses of the people. Since the First World War the economic and social changes in the area have brought into existence new classes and groups which have challenged the oligarchy's monopoly of political power, and have given rise to political parties and other civic groups capable of challenging not only the position of the landed and commercial aristocracy but also that of the armed forces as the ultimate arbiter of political affairs.

The period just before, during, and immediately after World War I saw a number of significant advances for the cause of democratic government in the Latin American countries. In Argentina, the election of the year 1916 brought to the presidency Hipólito Irigoyen, candidate of the Radical party, the spokesman for the middle classes and part of the working classes of that country. The victory of Irigoyen meant the abdication, for the time being at least, of the rural aristocrats who had dominated the country's government for nearly three quarters of a century. It meant also an era of political freedom which has not been matched in Argentina either before or since.

The Chilean presidential election of 1920 had much the same result. Arturo Alessandri, also the nominee of middle and working-class elements, was elected. His victory was the first step in transforming Chile from an oligarchic republic in which the rights of freedom of press, speech, and organization were safe enough, but actual participation in political activities was largely confined to a small group of landlords and urban upper- and middle-class elements, into a republic in which the masses of the people actively participated and had the final say through the ballot box in determining their administrators.

Uruguay, in the meanwhile, was engaged in one of the most interesting social and economic experiments in recent Latin American history. The election of José Batlle y Ordóñez to the presidency in 1903 put an end once and for all to a long period of chaotic strong-arm rule. His reelection in 1911 launched the country on a series of reforms which made Uruguay the model for the rest of the hemisphere for a whole generation. Under the leadership of Batlle y Ordóñez, Uruguay blazed paths for the hemisphere in social security and labor legislation, and in the use of government policy for the advancement of economic development.

Finally, the Mexican Revolution, begun in 1910, was sweeping away the semifeudal society which the country had inherited from colonial days. Agrarian reform had begun the process of placing ownership of the land in the hands of those who culti- vated it. A powerful labor movement was beginning to develop. The vast social, economic, and political transformation had begun which was to continue for at least two decades, and was to lay the foundations for economic growth, political stability, and a wide degree of democracy.

Some of the other nations of the area also seemed to be

evolving more slowly in the direction of a more or less democratic form of government. In always turbulent Cuba, in Paraguay, even in Peru, there was increased popular participation in the governmental process, and a degree of stability and democracy seemed to be emerging. The rest of Latin America, however, remained politically under the control of the traditional oligarchies, or languished under the latest in a long series of military dictatorships.

During the 1920's there were several important setbacks to the evolution of democracy in the hemisphere. Chile, in the grip of an economic crisis as the result of the decline of its principal industry, nitrate mining, and at the same time experiencing a profound social transformation, fell under the dictatorship of General Carlos Ibañez, who ruled from 1927 to 1931. Cuba's president, Gerardo Machado, elected as a representative of liberal middle-class interests, degenerated into one of the most brutal dictators of the time, under the pressure of a severe economic crisis. In Peru, the régime of Augusto B. Leguía, which also had aroused hopes of a democratic evolution at its inception, likewise was converted into a rigid dictatorship.

The decade of the 1930's opened with a series of revolutions. The fall of the Ibañez dictatorship in Chile, the Leguía régime in Peru, the Machado tyranny in Cuba, the overthrow of the oligarchical government in Brazil, were among the more hopeful upsets during this period. A severe reverse for democracy occurred, however, in Argentina, where President Hipólito Irigoyen, who had been reelected in 1928, was overthrown by a coalition of the army and the large landholders' Conservative party.

The revolutions which opened the decade of the 1930's did not bring any general movement in a democratic direction. The economic crisis after 1929 created difficulties for every government in the area, democratic or dictatorial. As a result, in most of the countries which had undergone upheavals, new dictatorships emerged. To understand the tenor of the times, one need only mention the Vargas régime in Brazil, which after 1937 engaged in the only avowedly Fascist experiment in the hemisphere; the series of governments which were made and unmade by Colonel Batista in Cuba; the Sánchez Cerro, Benavides, and Prado dictatorships in Peru; the thinly veiled military-Conservative dictatorship which dominated Argentina between 1930 and 1943. During the 1930's Argentina, Brazil, Paraguay, Bolivia, Peru, Ecuador, Venezuela, all of Central America except Costa Rica, Cuba, the Dominican Republic, and Haiti were all governed by dictatorships, or a succession of dictatorships.

However, certain advances were made during this period in Mexico, Colombia, and Chile. In the last of these, the overthrow of the Ibañez dictatorship in 1931 was followed by a period of rapidly changing governments, ending in the reelection of Arturo Alessandri as president late in 1932. Under his leadership, a degree of economic stability and political democracy was restored to that republic.

In Colombia the election of 1930 brought the triumph of the Liberal party for the first time in many decades. The peaceful transfer of power from the Conservatives attested to the strength of Colombian democracy at that time. The tempo of Colombian democracy quickened and, particularly during the administration of President Alfonso López (1934-1938), there was a rapid development of the trade union movement. Certain broad reforms were carried out, particularly in taxation policies and labor legislation.

Finally, in Mexico the decade of the 1930's saw the virtual completion of the structural changes coincident with the Mexican Revolution. Under President Lázaro Cárdenas, the agrarian reform program was all but completed; the peasants were brought into a much more active role in public affairs. At the same time, a series of local tyrants was ousted from power in a number of the states of the republic, and the last of the "private armies," which had threatened the stability of political life, was suppressed in 1938.

World War II and Its Aftermath

The Second World War had important political repercussions in Latin America. The Allied Powers carried on a vast amount of propaganda activity in the region, laying stress on the war as a fight for democracy and other high ideals. Virtually all the governments of the area, whether democratic or dictatorial, threw their lot in with the Allies. Two countries, Brazil and Mexico, actually sent troops to fight against the Germans and Japanese, and even in those countries which did not actively participate there was lively sympathy among great segments of the population for the fight against the Nazis and the Japanese warlords.

Even the Latin American dictators explained that they were aligned with the Allies to defend democracy against totalitarianism. Their words on this subject were frequently in glaring contrast to their actions at home. As time went on, as victory approached and enthusiasm for the Allied cause rose higher, the contrast between the words and the deeds of the Latin American dictators became increasingly apparent.

The upshot of this situation was that the dictators were soon on the defensive. Those first to topple were General Jorge Ubico Castañeda of Guatemala and General Maximiliano Hernández Martínez of El Salvador, who were forced out of office by civic uprisings in the middle of 1944. At almost the same time, President Fulgencio Batista presided over honest elections in Cuba, which gave the victory to the leader of the democratic Auténtico party, Dr. Ramón Grau San Martín.

Other dictators passed off the scene in rapid succession. Early in 1945 President Manuel Prado y Ugarteche was forced to hold elections in Peru, which were won by the opposition nominee,

José Bustamante y Rivero. At the same time, the country's majority party, the Partido Aprista, was legalized for the first time in a dozen years, and won a majority in the Senate and nearly a majority in the Chamber of Deputies.

A few months later President Getulio Vargas of Brazil, who had begun to loosen the reins of his dictatorship several months before, but was anxious to have himself rechosen in elections he had been obliged to call, was overthrown by the armed forces in October, 1945, when it began to appear as if the elections might not be held after all. General Eurico Dutra was chosen as president two months later, at which time a constitutional assembly was also elected to write a new basic document to supersede the Fascist corporate state which Vargas had fathered. The new democratic constitution went into effect in September, 1956.

In Venezuela the mild dictatorship of General Isaías Medina Angarita, who had allowed wide freedom of speech and organization, but refused to allow the free selection of his successor, was overthrown on October 18, 1945, by young army officers in conjunction with the country's majority political party, Acción Democrática. During the next three years, under the presidencies of Rómulo Betancourt and Rómulo Gallegos, three successive elections were held—for a constituent assembly, for president and congress, and for municipal officials. Freedom of political activity brought into existence several new political parties, and the régime launched a wide program of social reform and economic development.

Early in January, 1946, President Elie Lescot of Haiti, who had ruled with a strong hand, was overthrown by a civic-military uprising, when he sought illegally to have himself reelected. After a short interregnum, a schoolteacher, Dumarsais Estimé, was elected President of Haiti and the country enjoyed one of its few periods of relatively democratic government. Freedom of the press was protected, several political parties were organized, trade unionism was encouraged, and the government began to put into effect programs for extending the educational system, building public housing, and pushing forward the economic development of the nation.

Even those dictators who were not overthrown sought to bend with the democratic winds that were blowing. In Paraguay dictator Higinio Morínigo declared a general amnesty, allowed the legal reorganization of opposition political parties, freedom of the press and speech, and promised new elections. In Nicaragua President Anastasio Somoza considerably loosened the reins of his dictatorship, patronizing the development of a labor movement (under Communist control), and began making noises like a democrat. Much the same thing happened, though to a less extensive degree, in the Dominican Republic under dictator Rafael Leonidas Trujillo Molina.

The upshot of all these developments was that by the end of 1946 Mexico, Guatemala, Costa Rica, Panama, Colombia, Venezuela, Ecuador, Peru, Chile, Uruguay, Brazil, Cuba, and Haiti had democratic régimes. The dictatorship in Paraguay appeared on the way out; those of the Dominican Republic and Nicaragua seemed in difficulties; Bolivia had a government which gave hope of becoming more democratic; and El Salvador had a mild dictatorship which was a vast improvement over the brutal Martínez administration which had preceded it. Only the Carías Andino dictatorship in Honduras seemed impregnable, and only the newly installed Perón régime in Argentina seemed to be gaining momentum and to be on the offensive.

Trends in the Late 1940's and Early 1950's

The immediate post-World War II period was undoubtedly a high-water mark for democracy in Latin America. It was succeeded by almost a decade of reaction, during which one democratic government after another succumbed and was succeeded by a dictatorship.

Even during the period of democratic euphoria, there had been one glaring exception to the general trend, namely Argentina. There the Conservative party-army dictatorship of the 1930's and early 1940's had given way to the purely military régime installed on June 4, 1943, which in turn had paved the way for the emergence of a new kind of a Latin American dictator, Juan Domingo Perón.

Unlike most Latin American tyrants, whose civilian support has come from all or a faction of the economic and social upper classes, Perón's civilian backing came from the urban and rural working classes. Indeed, there is little doubt that during the late 1940's and early 1950's, Perón had the support of the majority of the people of Argentina.

Also in contrast with most of the Latin American dictators, who are merely interested in staying in power and enriching themselves, Perón attempted to evolve an ideology which would give a certain respectability and historical importance to his leadership. He did not want to be "just another Latin American dictator." He evolved a type of native totalitarianism which can take its place alongside Soviet communism, German Nazism, Italian Fascism, and Spanish Falangism.

Perón was ambitious to spread his influence throughout Latin America, and there is little doubt that his agents played a part in at least some of the *coups d'état* and other events which established dictatorships in many of the countries which at the end of World War II seemed to be on the road toward democratic government. This was particularly the case in Peru and Venezuela, where his military attachés were reported to have influenced the military men who overthrew the Bustamante and Gallegos governments. Argentine labor attachés also undoubtedly gave advice to the succeeding Odría and Pérez Jiménez dictatorships.

Paraguay was the first country in which the trend toward democracy was reversed. After a short period of political truce and of freedom of speech, press, and assembly, civil war broke out in that country early in 1947. The upshot of this was the reestablishment of a severe dictatorship, presided over successively by Natalicio González, Federico Chávez, and General Alfredo Stroessner. Each of these régimes was put in power by the armed forces, with the blessing of all or part of the so-called Colorado party. Under each of them, free speech and press were mere items in the constitution and no party except the Partido Colorado was allowed to function. Paraguayan exiles were spread liberally in all of the neighboring countries.

The democratic experiment in Peru came to a disastrous end in October, 1948. After an abortive naval mutiny in the port of Callao, the majority party, the Partido Aprista, was outlawed by President José Bustamante y Rivero. Three weeks later Bustamante y Rivero himself was ousted by a military coup led by General Manuel Odría. After two years of "provisional" rule, Odría had himself elected president, and he held on to that office until 1956.

Within less than a month after the fall of Bustamante's régime in Peru, the democratic government of President Rómulo Gallegos of Venezuela was overthrown by a military *coup d'état.* For four years the country was run by a three-man military junta (the first head of which, Colonel Carlos Delgado Chalbaud, was assassinated in 1950). After elections which turned out disastrously for the junta in December, 1952, one member of the junta, Colonel Marcos Pérez Jiménez, seized control, proclaimed himself provisional president, and had his puppet congress proclaim him "constitutional president" a month later. This military tyranny lasted until January, 1958.

Haiti's short flirtation with democracy came to an end in 1950 when President Estimé attempted to have the constitution changed to permit him to be reelected. He was succeeded by General Paul Magloire, who presided as a dictator for six years, falling when he too tried to reelect himself. After a period of turmoil, the country slid into still another dictatorship late in 1957.

The crisis of Colombian democracy was long and agonizing.

It began in 1946 when a split in the majority Liberal party opened the way for the election of Mariano Ospina Pérez, the Conservative candidate, to the presidency. A man of moderation, Ospina Pérez invited both parties to participate in his cabinet, which they did for almost two years.

Then in April, 1948, the country was thrown into terrible turmoil. First of all, the Liberals withdrew from the cabinet, on the occasion of the naming of Laureano Gómez, leader of the extreme right wing of the Conservative party, as Foreign Minister. A few days later, the idol of the Liberal party masses, Jorge Eliecer Gaitán, was assassinated, when coming out of his downtown Bogotá law office. His murder provoked a wild orgy of rioting by the largely Liberal populace of the city. Although the riots were brought to a halt by the reestablishment of a coalition government and the departure of Laureano Gómez for Spain, this truce lasted only a few months.

By early 1949 the Liberals had withdrawn again from the cabinet and civil war had broken out in large parts of the country, a civil war which was to last for almost ten years. Late in 1949 Laureano Gómez was elected president of Colombia in a poll in which the Liberals refused to take part. His régime was so much a strong-arm government that there was almost universal jubilation when Gómez was ousted by a military *coup d'état*, led by General Rojas Pinilla in June, 1953.

For about a year there was again a truce but it was brought to an end in the middle of 1954, when Rojas Pinilla had himself elected constitutional president by a constituent assembly whose members he had named himself. He continued to rule as a military dictator until May, 1957.

One of the most tragic reversions to dictatorship during this period was that of Cuba. Near the end of the Second World War, Cuba had had exemplary elections in which Dr. Ramón Grau San Martín, chief of the Auténtico party, was chosen as president. In 1948 free and reasonably honest elections were held once more, and Carlos Prío Socorrás, also an Auténtico, was elected to succeed Grau. The Cuban people were proud that their country seemed to be establishing a tradition of democratic transference of power.

Then in 1952 this tradition-in-the-making was brutally brushed aside. A presidential election was scheduled for June 1st of that year, and there were three candidates. The Auténtico party had named Carlos Hevía, an engineer and experienced politician; the Ortodoxo party, a split-off from the Auténticos, had named Dr. Roberto Agramonte, professor at the University of Havana; and ex-dictator Fulgencio Batista had named himself. There was considerable speculation concerning whether Hevía or Agramonte would win. There was universal agreement that Batista would not.

Nothing daunted, Fulgencio Batista presented himself early on the morning of March 10, 1952, at the principal army post, Camp Columbia, just outside of Havana. He gathered together a small group of junior officers and noncoms, and with their help arrested the top officers of the base. By daylight he had control of this important army installation. However, he gained control of the government largely through default, since President Carlos Prío Socorrás made little or no effort to rally the garrisons of Morro Castle and elsewhere on the island, which remained loyal, or to arm the students who were clamoring to defend the régime, or call the workers out on strike in defense of the duly constituted democratic government. By noon Batista was master of the situation.

One of the authors was in Havana a week after the Batista coup. He has seldom encountered such a feeling of frustration as was then general among the civilians of the Cuban capital. There was shock, resentment, and a feeling that absolutely nothing could be done about the situation.

With his coup Batista not only ended democratic government in Cuba, but he betrayed himself. By presiding over honest elections, and letting his worst enemy, Dr. Grau San Martín, win, he had established for himself an unequaled niche in the history of Cuba and Latin America. Seldom had dictators voluntarily given up power to a democratic régime. However, whatever aura of greatness this act may have created around him was completely dispelled by his complete thwarting of the wishes of the people on March 10, 1952.

Guatemala, too, succumbed to the trend toward dictatorship in this period. After the Revolution of 1944 elections had been held which resulted in Juan José Arevalo becoming president of the Republic. He presided over an essentially democratic administration. He launched a series of moderately advanced reforms, and seemed to be paving the way for democratic development in the largest Central American nation. However, he supported as his successor Colonel Jacobo Arbenz, who was strongly under the influence of the Communist party of Guatemala. During the year and a half of Arbenz's presidency, the country moved rapidly in the direction of a Communist dictatorship. It seems likely to the authors that if he had remained in power, Guatemala would have had a post-World War II type of "popular democracy" within six months to a year later.

The drift toward Communist dictatorship was stopped in 1954 by the establishment of the more traditional kind of military dictatorship. Colonel Carlos Castillo Armas, an exile in Honduras, organized an expedition—with help which still remains mysterious—to invade Guatemala. When the Guatemalan army virtually refused to fight Castillo Armas, Arbenz resigned, and a few days later Castillo Armas became for all practical purposes president of the republic. He organized an "election" later in the year in which participants voted by show of hands, and he won by a 99 per cent majority.

The Castillo Armas régime, in spite of the good intentions of the president, was a brutal dictatorship. Hundreds and perhaps thousands of peasants and workers were killed in a wave of revenge on the part of employers and landlords, who felt that they had been mistreated during the Arevalo-Arbenz period. The agrarian reform program started under Arbenz was reversed, and virtually all opposition was forbidden.

In contrast to the countries which had succumbed to dictatorship between 1947 and 1955, there were only three Latin American nations in which democracy made notable progress. These were Bolivia, Costa Rica, and Ecuador.

A new epoch in Bolivian history opened on April 9, 1952, when an armed insurrection led by the Movimiento Nacionalista Revolucionario began in La Paz and provincial cities and towns. This uprising, which lasted three days, marked the beginning of the Bolivian national revolution.

The MNR government in the following years began a vast program of social, economic, and political reform. Fundamental was the decree of August 2, 1953, which declared an agrarian reform, turning the land back to the Indians from whom it had been seized and stolen during the four centuries or more since the coming of the white man. Other notable acts were the nationalization of the country's chief source of foreign exchange, the tin mines; the launching of an extensive program of economic development; the expansion of the educational system, especially in the countryside; and the granting of the franchise to illiterates, thus making the Indians a part of the civic life of the nation.

During the four-year administration of Victor Paz Estenssoro, 1952 to 1956, the MNR did not treat its political opponents in a democratic fashion. To a considerable degree this was the result of the fact that these opponents still believed that the way to change governments in Bolivia was by *coup d'état* and devoted much of their energies to putting this belief into practice—albeit unsuccessfully. In part, however, it must be admitted that the Paz Estenssoro régime dealt more harshly with its opponents than even these conditions would have justified.

The administration of Hernán Siles Zuazo, elected in 1956 as candidate of the Movimiento Nacionalista Revolucionario, sought to change this policy. It established a wide degree of freedom of the press and of speech. It offered amnesty to the opponents of the administration on the condition that they give up attempts to overthrow the MNR government by force. Certainly the democratic atmosphere of the Siles Zuazo régime was a marked improvement over that of Paz Estenssoro and most of its predecessors.

The real significance of the MNR revolution is that it has laid the groundwork for the real development of democracy in Bolivia. Before April 9, 1952, three fourths of the population—the Indians—were kept completely out of civic affairs, and, in fact, lived under semiservile conditions. The main accomplishment of the Bolivian national revolution to date is the freeing of the Indian from these bonds and the beginning of his integration into the political affairs of the nation. Through the enfranchisement of the Indian, the granting of the land to the peasants, which will give them a solid economic base, and the revolutionary government's program of economic development, the absolutely necessary preconditions for political democracy were established. The future of democracy in Bolivia will henceforward depend at least as much upon the opposition's acceptance of constitutional democratic methods of political activity as upon the attitude of the government.

As a result of all of these events, by the beginning of 1955 a majority of the countries of Latin America were in the hands of dictators. Those which were without question dictatorships were Argentina, Colombia, Cuba, the Dominican Republic, Guatemala, Haiti, Honduras, Nicaragua, Paraguay, Peru, and Venezuela—eleven in all. El Salvador was run by a mild dictatorship which seemed to be in the process of moving in a democratic direction. Only Bolivia, Brazil, Chile, Costa Rica, Ecuador, Mexico, Panama, and Uruguay were more or less firmly in the democratic column.

The Democratic Recovery in the Late 1950's

Just as the Perón triumph in Argentina was of key importance in the general resurgence of dictatorships in the late 1940's, so his overthrow in September, 1955, was crucial in the reversal of this process in the late 1950's. After the ouster of Perón, the dictatorships of Odría in Peru, Rojas Pinilla in Colombia, Lozano in Honduras, Pérez Jiménez in Venezuela, and Batista in Cuba fell within a period of less than three and a half years.

The circumstances surrounding the fall of these tyrants differed in each case. However, a universal theme running through all of them was the determined and valiant resistance of democratic elements even in the face of what seemed to be hopeless odds. In the following four chapters we shall look in some detail at this democratic resurgence, which gives some hope at least that the era of strong-arm dictatorships may be drawing to a close in Latin America.

CHAPTER FIVE

SOME RECENT
DEMOCRATIC VICTORIES
PART ONE:
THE FALL OF PERÓN

Juan Domingo Perón set a new style for Latin American
dictators. He was not a mere tyrant placed in office by the army.
Instead, he owed his ten years in power to a novel coalition of
organized workers and military men. His régime was revolutionary in a real sense. It transferred power from one group in
society to another. Unlike most Latin American dictators, Perón
kept the loyalty of a large part of his nation's citizens long after
he was out of office and out of the country.

There is no doubt that Perón at one time enjoyed the support
of the majority of the people of Argentina. His appeal to them
was twofold: social and nationalistic. During the years when he
was on his way to power and was serving as Secretary of Labor
(1943-1945), Perón won the sympathy of the majority of the
working class because he was the first powerful government
figure in two decades or more who had demonstrated any real
interest in the welfare of the urban and rural wage earners of
Argentina. Furthermore, he brought about real gains for the

74

workers during that period. He brought sizable real wage increases, by forcing employers to negotiate favorable collective agreements with their employees' unions. He decreed an extensive body of social and labor legislation. He encouraged the growth of the trade union movement, so that when he left office it was at least four to five times the size it had been when he appeared on the scene in 1943.

Most important of all, Perón gave to the workers of Argentina a feeling of dignity and a sense of actually participating in the affairs of the nation which they had never previously possessed. Perhaps it was this fact rather than the material gains which he brought about in the beginning (many of which proved to be fleeting), which won him the wide popular backing that he undoubtedly possessed.

There is also little doubt that the Perón régime was evolving a native type of totalitarianism. The freedom of expression and action of the opposition was more and more circumscribed, and all elements of the population were being regimented in parastate organizations which would direct not only economic activities but all other phases of life. The cult of the leader was assiduously and even garishly propagated. Had Perón remained in power for a sufficient length of time, he undoubtedly would have evolved as completely strait-jacketed a régime as the European Fascists and Communists had installed in their respective nations.

One of the inevitable results of the totalitarian proclivities of Perón was that he clashed with the Catholic Church. Although he had had the support of the Church hierarchy during the election campaigns of 1946 and 1951, by 1954 relations between the two had become cold, and Perón launched his famous attack upon the Church, which was one of the prime causes of disaffection with his administration, particularly among officers of the armed forces.

The third significant thing about the Perón phenomenon was that Juan Domingo Perón chose to be a dictator. He won the election of 1946 with a majority which gave him almost two thirds of the members of the lower house of Congress, and all but two of the senatorial seats. He had solid popular support. He could have stayed in power for a long period of time without using repressive methods against his opponents. However, he did not choose to be a democrat. Rather he riveted on the country a dictatorship which grew in its arbitrariness and brutality the longer he stayed in power.

In the fourth place, the Perón régime brought about the definitive transfer of political power from the rural oligarchy which had dominated Argentina for a century (with the short interregnum of the Radical tenure in office from 1916 to 1930), to the urban middle and working classes. Although he did not deprive the landlords of their land, he did take out of their hands the sale of their produce, creating a government monopoly to purchase and sell the country's principal agricultural and grazing products, while at the same time forcing up rural labor costs by social security and labor legislation and effective agrarian trade unionism.

On the other hand, Perón encouraged industrialization, creating special banks to extend credit to new industries and for the extension of old ones. He reversed the country's traditional low tariff policies, and extended considerable protection to industry.

Weaknesses of the Perón Régime

Indeed, Perón went too far in these policies, at least insofar as squeezing the agriculturalists was concerned. The net result was a catastrophic decline in the area of land under cultivation and the amount of grain and meat produced. The Peronistas seemed to feel that somehow or other the nation's economy could be diversified and strengthened by the country's ceasing to be an exporter of grains and grazing products to Europe. This crisis in agriculture was one of the causes of the economic difficulties which helped to bring down the régime.

Another error of the Peronista economic policy was the failure to use a part of the foreign exchange reserves which it had available right after World War II to recapitalize parts of the economy which were in disrepair. The railroads, agricultural equipment, and various other parts of the nation's capital equipment needed replacement, but Perón did little to procure the necessary capital goods. The upshot was that the Argentine economy became increasingly inefficient.

Perón himself realized by the early 1950's that the economic policies he had been following were having drastic results. Using the excuse of a visit by Dr. Milton Eisenhower to Argentina in the middle of 1953, he suddenly reversed his policy of violent attacks upon the United States, and began actively to seek help from the United States government and private business interests in this country. One result was a $60,000,000 loan from the Export-Import Bank early in 1955 for the construction of a large steel plant in San Nicolás, in the Province of Buenos Aires.

The principal fruit of Perón's courting of United States business interests was a contract with the Standard Oil Company of California. This contract gave the company oil exploration and drilling concessions in the southern part of the country under conditions which resulted in howls of protest from all Argentine nationalists, and even made his own puppet congress hesitate about giving the contract their approval. This incident added large piles of fuel to the growing fire against Perón.

Finally, it should be noted that the alliance upon which the government was based, that of the army and the trade union movement, had always been somewhat precarious. Plots and counterplots among the military had been one of Perón's constant preoccupations. There had always been officers who resented the important position given to labor in the Perón spectrum. There were others who were shocked by what they regarded as extreme social policies. Still others objected to the antidemocratic aspects of the government, while some were dubious about the frank way in which Perón had dragged the army into party politics. Finally, there were always important officers who were merely jealous of Perón, and felt that their capabilities and genius for ruling were as great as those of the dictator.

The Movement to Overthrow Perón

Elements of the armed forces moved against Perón twice during 1955. On June 16 important parts of the navy, including its air force, rose in revolt, strafed the presidential palace and the Plaza de Mayo, and came within an ace of upsetting the government. They failed because army groups committed to the revolt withdrew at the last moment.

For the next three months, Perón relaxed somewhat the rigidity of his rule. He bid for a "truce" with the political opposition, and maneuvered to oust all of those in the armed forces whose loyalty he doubted. On August 31, he seemed to have reestablished his government on a firm basis. He addressed a crowd of a hundred thousand people in the Plaza de Mayo, and urged them to kill anyone who attempted to "get in our way." He is said to have looked at a group of army officers who were standing at his side as he said this.

However, within two weeks another military revolt flared. This time, the whole navy joined in, seized most of the country's naval bases, and sailed up to the Buenos Aires area, threatening to bomb the city if Perón did not surrender. Meanwhile, army and air force units in Córdoba and in the Northeastern province of Corrientes, joined the uprising. After several days of bitter fighting the rebels finally won in the Córdoba region, and by that time Perón had fled to a Paraguayan gunboat which was opportunely anchored in Buenos Aires harbor.

The group which had joined in the effort to overthrow Perón was heterogeneous in nature. They can perhaps be divided into three groups: the anti-Peronista political parties which had fought against the régime consistently since 1943; civilian elements which had once supported Perón but had broken with him at one time or another over the years, including strongly Catholic elements, extreme nationalists, and people who might best be classified as "neo-Peronistas"; and the armed forces.

The anti-Peronista political parties had never ceased in their struggle against the dictatorship. Five groups were of principal importance. In the lead numerically were the members and leaders of the Radical party (Unión Cívica Radical). Although badly split among themselves, they were united against Perón. Second in importance were the Socialists, who had been particularly persecuted by the deposed dictator. Third were the Conservatives, the group ousted by the 1943 *coup d'état* which paved the way for Perón. Fourth was the small Progressive Democratic party, the strength of which was largely confined to the Province of Santa Fé. Finally, there were the Christian Democrats, a new party, the establishment of which in the last years of the Perón administration was one of the causes of the dictator's violent feud with the Church.

These parties were united in their desire to see the quickest possible reestablishment of a democratic, civilian government. As time passed, however, they began to quarrel violently among themselves concerning the best way to bring about such an event, and the appropriate manner for dealing with the Peronistas, who still constituted a large segment of the population.

The ex-Peronistas, right-wing Catholics, extreme nationalists, and neo-Peronistas, although heterogeneous, constituted in the first months after the fall of Perón a strong group, with a program which differed from that of the other civilians. They generally were for a "soft" approach to the Peronistas, sought to renew the extreme nationalist policies which Perón had abandoned toward the end, and sought to strengthen the political position of the Church.

The armed forces, which had borne the brunt of the final battle against the dictator and which had the ultimate control of the government which succeeded Perón, were likewise violently split among themselves. The navy and a large part of the air force took an utterly uncompromising position not only against Perón but against the Peronistas. The army was riddled with factions and for the two and a half years, between the fall of Perón and the inauguration of a constitutional régime once again, was forced into a position secondary to that of the other military groups.

The first government to take over after Perón's abdication was headed by General Eduardo Lonardi, who had led the uprising in the Córdoba region. He was seconded by Vice Admiral Isaac Rojas, who became vice president of the provisional government. Lonardi included in his cabinet and among his advisors representatives of all the military factions and of both groups of civilians. He established a Consultative Junta as a kind of interim Congress, which was made up of representatives of all important civilian groups and was presided over by Admiral Rojas.

The Lonardi government followed a moderate policy insofar as the followers of the deposed dictator were concerned. Although Hugo de Pietri, the secretary general of the General Confederation of Labor at the time of Perón's ouster, was forced out of office, other Peronistas remained in charge of that powerful organization. Lonardi and his Minister of Labor hoped that by calling new elections in all of the unions and in the General Confederation of Labor (CGT) within one hundred twenty days, the workers themselves would oust most of the more corrupt and vicious Peronista trade union leaders.

General Lonardi himself proclaimed that "There are no vanquished and no victors." However, he did outlaw the Peronista party, and made it clear that Perón himself would not be allowed to take part again in the country's political life. He also took an important step when he allowed the Standard Oil of California contract to lapse by not ratifying it by the October 31, 1955, deadline called for in the document itself.

The Lonardi régime was torn between the two civilian groups. For about two months he succeeded in keeping the two forces balanced in his administration. However, when on November 9 he made changes in his cabinet which seemed to give decisive control to the ex-Peronista, nationalist group, all but two members of the Consultative Junta resigned. Two days later, a *coup d'état* by an army group headed by General Pedro Eugenio Aramburu and supported by the navy under Admiral Rojas, ousted General Lonardi from the presidency. He died of cancer a few months later.

The Aramburu Provisional Government

The triumph of Aramburu's coup meant that the pendulum had swung definitely on the side of the anti-Peronista parties. However, the new leadership was faced with an immediate crisis when the labor movement, still under Peronista control, declared a revolutionary general strike. This was quickly crushed, and President Aramburu and his new Minister of Labor, Dr. Raúl Migone, declared the "intervention" of the General Confederation of Labor and of all of its constituent unions. "Interventors" or receivers were put in charge of virtually every union in the country, and most of these men were chosen from the ranks of the armed forces officers' corps.

The Aramburu régime also took other stern measures against the Peronistas. Virtually all the Peronista members of Congress and the state legislatures under the dictatorship who had not escaped from the country were jailed, pending hearings, as were many of the top trade union officials. Others who had held more or less important positions during the Perón era felt it politic to go into hiding.

President Aramburu and Vice President Rojas were pledged to the restoration of a democratic, civilian government through free elections, and they held to this objective in spite of tremendous pressure from elements who would have liked to see the military-dominated régime stay in power more or less indefinitely. They also pledged that no one who held office during their tenure—including themselves—would run for office when general elections were held. This promise they kept to the letter.

These two men, particularly Aramburu, were remarkable military figures. They honestly believed that the armed forces should get out of politics and turn the running of the government over to civilians who had been duly chosen by the people. Aramburu on various occasions—most notably in his farewell address to the armed forces shortly before giving up the presidency—admitted frankly that the military bore much of the responsibility for the difficulties through which Argentina had suffered during the previous quarter century or more. They were responsible, he said, for the original ouster of the elected Irigoyen government in 1930, which served as a precedent for the 1943 revolt, which was also almost solely an armed forces responsibility. It was high time, Aramburu added, for the armed forces to repair the damage they had wrought and "return to the barracks."

The Aramburu-Rojas leadership was faced with many serious and almost insoluble problems. One of these was the constant threat of subversion by pro-Peronista elements and by ambitious members of the armed services. The most challenging crisis of this nature was an attempted uprising on June 9, 1956, which was quickly suppressed, and as a result of which one general, several other officers, and numerous enlisted men and civilians were executed. Thereafter, there were fewer problems of a subversive nature.

The economic situation, however, continued to deteriorate. The economic policies of Perón had brought the nation to the verge of a first-rate crisis. Through excessively harsh measures against agriculture he had reduced the country's output of its principal export products to a disastrous degree. His demagoguery bore prime responsibility for a notable though incalcu-

able decline in the productivity of urban labor. He left the country with a foreign exchange deficit, a sizable foreign debt, a
run-down transportation system, and a creeping inflation which
was beginning to gallop.

Aramburu attempted to deal with this problem, though with
only modest success. His principal weapon was control of wages.
Although Aramburu decreed a general 10 per cent wage increase
on February 1, 1956, when existing collective contracts expired,
he postponed any further increases as long as possible. However,
by the beginning of 1957, all the government's efforts proved
futile, and the régime was forced to grant very considerable increases to various workers' groups.

Aramburu also sought to stimulate an increase in production,
largely by declaring a policy of "free enterprise" under which
prices were not controlled, and those government and collective
bargaining measures which employers felt limited output were
relaxed or abolished. Considerably higher prices were offered to
agriculturalists, and the process of getting the government out
of the purchase and sale of the country's principal agricultural
export products was begun.

Finally, the government sought to get help from abroad for
the recapitalization of those parts of the economy in which capital
equipment was decrepit or worn out, particularly the railways.
A loan of $100,000,000 was contracted from the United States
Export-Import Bank, most of which was to be spent on railway
equipment and rolling stock, and much of the rest on the impor-
tation of needed agricultural equipment. Some other smaller
loans were also made.

These economic measures, particularly the attempt to hold
wages in check, and the policy of letting prices rise, served to
arouse a great deal of discontent among the working class. The
workers were inclined to be hostile toward the government in
any case, since they felt that the September, 1955, revolution had
ousted the man who was their best friend, Perón. They tended

to feel that the Aramburu government was the representative of employer interests, and this belief seemed to be confirmed by the economic policies of the administration.

Working-class discontent was intensified by Aramburu's policies with regard to the trade unions. Although the "intervention" in the labor movement was probably essential at the time it occurred, in November, 1955, because of the attempt by the trade union leadership to oust the Aramburu régime by force, the government undoubtedly made the situation worse subsequently. For one thing, the Ministry of Labor was almost completely out of touch with what the workers—even those hostile to Perón—were thinking and feeling. Minister of Labor Migone, though an expert on international labor law, had been in exile for more than a decade, and even when living in Argentina had not been particularly closely associated with the labor movement.

Furthermore, Migone refused to take into his confidence and work with those elements in the labor movement which had been opposed to Perón. He argued, correctly, that these people were for the most part associated with one or another of the anti-Peronista political parties, and, therefore, were interested in labor affairs from a political, not a trade union, point of view. The labor movement must become apolitical, Migone maintained. However, he failed to realize that the problem facing Argentina at that moment was not whether the trade union movement was to be under political influences—it was inevitable that it would remain so for some time—but rather under what political influence it was going to fall. The anti-Peronista trade union leaders of various kinds were the only ones who were adequately equipped to give battle to the Peronistas in the unions themselves.

The upshot of all this was that the Ministry of Labor did not have friendly relations with any element in the labor movement. Rather, it tended to be staffed in its upper and middle ranks either by military men, or by the "bright young men" from the personnel departments of the country's biggest industries. It is understandable that the workers felt that they had no friends in he Ministry, and that it was serving the interests of their employers.

In addition, the government took more time than was advisable to restore the autonomy of the trade union movement. For almost a year most of the trade unions of Argentina were administered by military officers. During this period, the workers tended to feel themselves helpless and without any protection. Their unions were ineffective, and in the hands of people who knew little about the worker's problems, and the Ministry was, the workers felt, in absolutely hostile hands.

Factionalism in the Anti-Peronista Parties

These problems in the military, economic, and labor fields were all complicated by political developments. Although the anti-Peronista parties remained rather closely united during the two months of the Lonardi régime, deep splits developed subsequently within the Radical, Socialist, Conservative, and Progressive Democratic parties. Basically, these divisions of opinion were the result of different concepts of how to deal with the Peronistas.

One group in each of these parties felt that no compromise whatsoever could be made with the rank and file of the Peronistas. It was necessary to "educate" them to the effect that Perón was responsible for all the country's miseries, but no attempt should be made to meet them halfway. Therefore, they argued, it was necessary to give virtually uncritical allegiance to the government, not even to criticize it publicly when it was wrong in its policies.

The other group in each of these parties felt that the fundamental need was to win over a considerable segment of the Peronista rank and file, so that the country would cease to be divided almost equally between supporters and opponents of the deposed dictator. In order to do this, it was necessary to assure the workers in no uncertain terms that the provisional government intended actually to extend the labor and social legislation inaugurated by Perón, and wanted to be friendly to the labor movement. These people also argued that when the Aramburu government made mistakes in the social and labor field, it should be criticized for these mistakes.

The general position of this second type of group in the old anti-Peronista parties led them to oppose to an increasing degree many of the policies of the government. They urged the quick restoration of autonomy to the trade unions even if this meant that many of them would fall once again into the hands of the Peronistas. They urged a wide amnesty for imprisoned Peronistas, particularly those who had been active in the labor movement and against whom no specific charges of corruption or other misconduct had been filed. These elements also attacked the government's "free enterprise" economic policy, and severely criticized any moves which seemed to indicate an abatement of the strident nationalism which had been such a characteristic feature under Perón.

These differences of opinion brought about splits in the Conservative and Progressive Democratic parties, each of which broke up into two distinct organizations. The schism in the Socialist ranks did not take an organizational form until after the inauguration of a new constitutional president, but the two rival factions were virtually unable to converse with each other by the end of the provisional régime.

The most important split, however, took place in the ranks of the Radical party. Even under Perón the party had been divided into the two basic elements we have mentioned, with various subgroupings in each of them. On the side of an unremitting policy against the Peronistas were the so-called "Unionistas." Favoring a more flexible approach to the supporters of the ex dictator were the so-called "Intransigentes," who were split into two competing elements which worked together so long as Perón was president, but split apart once he had been overthrown.

The leader of the Intransigentes was Arturo Frondizi, who ha been a member of the Chamber of Deputies early in the Perón administration, was the party's candidate for vice president in the 1951 election, and about two years before Perón's fall was elected president of the Radical party. He made no secret of his desire to be elected president of the republic at the end of the provisional régime.

The Reestablishment of Constitutional Government

The Aramburu régime was pledged to reestablish constitutional government. The Radicals held their nominating convention for president and vice president in November, 1956. Arturo Frondizi was named to run for the presidency and a teacher and lawyer from Rosario, Alejandro Gómez, was his running mate. However, a month later the Intransigentes, who had dominated the Radicals' nominating convention, split. A large segment led by Ricardo Balbín, 1951 Radical candidate for president, and Amadeo Sabattini, the "grand old man" of the Intransigente ranks, joined with the Unionistas to form the Unión Cívica Radical del Pueblo (People's Radical Party). The Frondizi forces then reorganized as the Unión Cívica Radical Intransigente.

In 1957 President Aramburu called elections in July for a constituent assembly. The Aramburu government had suspended the 1949 Perón constitution and had reinstated the older one of 1853. However, it was universally agreed that the 1853 document was out of date and needed modification, particularly with regard to social and economic matters.

These elections were the first test of strength after the fall of Perón. They showed that the fallen dictator still had a large following. He instructed his followers to cast blank votes with the result that a larger number of blank ballots were cast than were received for any party. The People's Radicals came in second, the Intransigente Radicals third. The Socialists, Christian Democrats, and other smaller parties were far behind the three top groups.

The constituent assembly was abortive. The Intransigente Radicals and several small groups walked out in the early phases of the meeting, as they had promised to do during the election campaign, on the grounds that the provisional government was acting unconstitutionally in calling a constitutional convention. When the Unión Cívica Independiente, a small group pledged to extreme "free enterprise" also walked out, the assembly was left without a quorum.

Shortly afterward, President Aramburu summoned elections for president, vice president, members of the Senate and Chamber of Deputies, members of all provincial legislatures as well as governors and all elected municipal officials. From the beginning, the contest for president was between Arturo Frondizi of the Intransigente Radicals and Ricardo Balbín, named by the Unión Cívica Radical del Pueblo. However, in addition, nominees were put forward by the Socialists, two Conservative factions, several groups of neo-Peronistas, the Christian Democrats, the Unión Cívica Independiente, and various other groups. Several other smaller parties, including the Communists and extreme nationalists, threw their support to Frondizi, for reasons best known to themselves.

It remained unclear for a considerable period of time what position Perón would take in the electoral contest. He was barred by the provisional government from being a candidate, and the Peronista party as such was not permitted to reorganize openly. However, Perón stood to lose a good deal if he again instructed his supporters to vote in blank as they had done in August, 1957, because many of them might not do so. In any case, the only way out for the Peronistas was to get in office a régime which would allow them to resume open political activity.

On February 3, 1958, the exiled dictator dispatched a letter to his followers instructing them to vote for Frondizi. He thus probably saved his own political position, and he assured Frondizi a victory of such proportions that it could not be challenged. Although Frondizi would probably have won with out Perón's support, his victory would have been by so narrow a margin that those in the armed forces who were urging that he not be allowed to take office would perhaps have gotten their way.

Elected on February 23, 1958, Arturo Frondizi was inaugurated on May 1. With his inauguration, the first civilian president to hold office in fifteen years took office. Although Frondizi's difficulties had only begun with his inauguration, this event meant that Argentina was back on the democratic road once again.

Although Frondizi had been elected on a platform promising the continuation of the social and nationalist policies of Perón, he very soon became aware of the fact that the first need was to restore the nation's economy. Thus, though he paid off political debts from the campaign by giving government posts to nationalists and neo-Peronistas, and by giving legal authorization for the first time in seventy-five years to Catholic-controlled universities, he completely reversed the economic policies which he had advocated while a candidate.

Frondizi threw open Argentina's doors to foreign investors, even allowing them once again into the very controversial petroleum industry, from which they had been barred for thirty years. At the same time, he attempted to hold down wages, after giving an initial 60 per cent wage increase late in May, 1958. He refused to allow the reestablishment of the General Confederation of Labor, and followed the policies of Perón and Aramburu of intervening frequently in the internal affairs of the trade union movement. Concurrently he followed a policy of encouraging agricultural interests.

Frondizi topped these actions by adopting a stringent "austerity" program, which involved freeing prices and attempting to freeze wages at the same time. He sought to balance the government budget by raising rates on the railroads and other government-owned enterprises so as to reduce their deficits. This program had as one of its most spectacular effects the forcing up of the price of meat to the point where the tremendously carnivorous Argentines could afford it only a couple times a week, thus cutting down consumption and reserving more cattle for breeding purposes and for export.

The austerity program was enacted in conformity with demands made by the International Monetary Fund, as its price for extensive financial aid. At the same time it went into effect, the Fund and the United States government extended loans and grants of $328,000,000 to the Argentine government, to be used for exchange stabilization and for projects for reequipment of Argentine industry, agriculture, and transportation. At the end of 1959 a further $200,000,000 was advanced to the Frondizi régime.

The program of Frondizi aroused widespread unrest among both civilians and the military. Long and bitter strikes were frequent, and the government crushed them relentlessly. Much of the press violently attacked the government, and virtually all political elements joined the opposition, including large segments of Frondizi's own Unión Cívica Radical Intransigente. In July, 1959, military pressure resulted in a reorganization of Frondizi's cabinet, and the installation as virtual prime minister, with full authority in the economic sphere, of Alvaro Alzogaray, head of the extreme free enterprise party, Unión Cívica Independiente.

As this is being written, Frondizi remains in power, and his country continues to suffer the aftermath of the damage which Perón did to Argentina's economy and civic life. Frondizi continues to argue that by the end of his presidential term, his program will reestablish the soundness of the economy and enable a beginning to be made on the program of economic development and extended social legislation which he preached as a candidate. It will take all Frondizi's admitted intelligence, skill as a politician, and ability to size up coldly the needs of his country, his party, and himself to assure that Argentina's fragile democratic structure will remain intact.

CHAPTER SIX

SOME RECENT
DEMOCRATIC VICTORIES
PART TWO:
PERU, COLOMBIA, AND HONDURAS

The fall of Perón acted like a detonator to set off a series of
upsets of dictatorial régimes in various parts of the hemisphere.
It gave heart to the opponents of dictatorship elsewhere and
removed the only dictatorship with any popular backing. Three
of the earliest victories for democracy were in Peru, Colombia,
and Honduras.

The Odría Government in Peru

General Manuel Odría had seized power at the end of
October, 1948, in a military uprising against which the elected
president, José Bustamante y Rivero, was unable to protect himself. After two years as provisional president, General Odría
formalized and "constitutionalized" his situation by having himself "elected" in 1950 in a poll in which the only opposing candidate allowed to participate withdrew, charging fraud, before
election day.

Odría's régime was merely the latest in a long series of similar dictatorships in Peru. Like its predecessors, it rested upon the bayonets of the army, and upon the support it received from the oligarchic interests which have traditionally dominated the country's economy—the large landholders, bankers, and important merchants. It enjoyed little popular support among the masses of the people though Odría, apparently on Perón's suggestion, made certain gestures toward ingratiating himself with the urban workers by extending the country's social legislation and building some low-cost housing.

The Apristas

Political activity was extremely limited under Odría. The majority party, the Partido Aprista Peruano, which had fought against successive dictatorships in Peru since 1930, was outlawed, its leading members were forced into exile, or were jailed. The top figure in the party, Victor Raúl Haya de la Torre, sought refuge in the Colombian Embassy in January, 1949, but the Odría government refused to follow the normal procedure in such cases, and allow him to go abroad. For over four years Haya remained a virtual prisoner in the Colombian Embassy, until foreign pressure finally forced Odría to agree to allow him to leave.

The Partido Aprista is one of the most vigorous and valiant fighters in the Latin American struggle for democracy. It was the pioneer of a group of parties in Latin America which have played a key part in this struggle during the last quarter of a century or more. Emerging out of an alliance between university students and the organized labor movement immediately after World War I, the Aprista Movement was formally organized as a political party after the downfall of the dictatorship of President Augusto B. Leguía in 1930.

In exile in the 1920's, the founder of the party, Victor Raúl

Haya de la Torre, and his close associates had sought to evolve an ideology which would be particularly appropriate to Latin America, or "Indo America" as they called it. They rejected the Socialist and Communist doctrines, which they claimed were evolved to suit industrial Europe, not semifeudal, semicolonial America.

The Apristas developed their own distinctive philosophy. They advocated an alliance among those classes in Peru and other Latin American countries which had interests naturally opposed to the old régime, that is, the urban wage-earning class, the middle class, the intellectuals, and the peasantry. These groups, they felt, should support a program of social legislation, spread education, and, most important of all, agrarian reform.

The Apristas argued that economic development and industrialization needed the cooperation of the government, native industrialists, and even foreign investors. However, they believed that the old-style foreign investment, which merely sought to exploit local resources for the benefit of the highly industrialized nations, which enjoyed special privileges, and which frequently called upon its home government for support—sometimes to the point of military intervention—should no longer be tolerated.

Thus the Apristas advocated general government direction of the process of industrialization and development. In addition, they were "anti-imperialist," insisting that foreign investors should be welcomed only when they conformed to the laws of the country, when they forswore appeals to their home governments, and when their investments contributed to the general development of the national economy.

The Aprista party was illegal during most of the period from its organization in 1930 until 1956. Only for short periods in 1930-1931, 1933-1934, and between 1945 and 1948 was it allowed to function openly. The rest of the time it was kept outside the law by the successive dictatorships which ruled the country. However, upon numerous occasions, it was able to demonstrate that it was the party representing the majority of the Peruvians. In 1936 it elected a president, only to have the ballot counting stopped by dictator Benavides, who had his puppet congress "extend" his term for three more years. In 1945 the votes of the Apristas elected José Bustamante y Rivero, who presided over one of the few interregnums of democracy in Peruvian history.

Political Conditions Under Odría

General Odría's régime was a thinly-veiled military dictatorship. Generals and colonels held many of the cabinet posts, and the rest were filled by representatives of the traditional oligarchy. With the Aprista party outlawed, the only party which was allowed to put up a semblance of opposition was the tiny Socialist party, which was permitted to have one senator and two or three members of the Chamber of Deputies.

In spite of Odría's pretense at a "social" program, the trade union movement was not permitted to function freely. Most of the country's unions, particularly in the interior, were suppressed, and although some in the vicinity of Lima and in the oil fields around Talara were permitted to function, they did so only under close surveillance of the Ministry of Labor and the police. Frequently, trade union leaders were called in, shown their Aprista party membership cards which had been captured by the police, and were threatened with jail or worse if they persisted in pushing their unions' demands.

For two years most of the important union leaders were jailed. After they were released in 1950 the government impeded every move to reestablish the Confederation of Workers of Peru (Confederación de Trabajadores del Perú) and most of its affiliated national industrial unions and regional federations. Several times the government attempted to foist Communist leaders on the Confederation when attempts were made to reorganize it, and when the union leaders refused to accept the Communists, the government banned the reestablishment of the CTP.

At the beginning, the Odría dictatorship had the support of virtually all the traditional landlord-mercantile-banking oligarchy. However, when disagreements arose between President Odría and one element among the oligarchy, led by newspaper publisher Pedro Beltrán and ex-President Manuel Prado y Ugarteche, Odría made short shrift of these civilians' opposition. Beltrán was jailed for some time, his principal editor, Eudosio Ravines, was exiled, and generally the supporters of Beltrán were maltreated.

The Election of 1956

As the end of President Odría's term of office approached, a crisis arose in the régime early in 1956. General Odría made overtures to secure his own reelection, and certain generals who aspired to the succession were suddenly found to be involved in "plots" against the president and were dismissed. However, sizable segments of the officer corps joined with elements of the oligarchy to put a veto on General Odría's desire to succeed himself. They demanded that elections be held to name a successor.

The resulting election campaign was a complicated one. The first candidate in the lists was a civilian engineer, Hernán Lavalle, who enjoyed the blessings of Odría. At first it appeared as if the ground were being prepared for the more or less automatic "election" of Lavalle.

However, there suddenly appeared a second candidate, an architect and professor at San Marcos University in Lima, Fernando Belaúnde Terry, who had been a deputy during the democratic hiatus of 1945-1948, when he had been closely allied with the Apristas. He now appeared as a "popular" opponent to the government's apparent attempt to impose its own choice on the country, and was able to arouse a good deal of genuine support among students, professional people, and some elements of the urban working class.

Finally, a few weeks before the election, still a third candidate appeared. This was ex-President Manuel Prado y Ugarteche, one of the richest men in Peru, who had been a dictator during his earlier presidential term, and who at the beginning of his campaign seemed to have no possibility at all of victory.

As had happened on various occasions in the past, the outcome of the election came to depend on the Aprista party. Although it was outlawed, it still had the support of a large part of the voting populace, and its backing was enough to give the margin of victory to whichever candidate it supported.

All three nominees bid for the endorsement of The Partido Aprista. One of the principal leaders of the party, Ramiro Prialé, had returned secretly from exile and had begun the work of reorganizing the party in various parts of the country. Odría and his candidate Lavalle soon entered into contact with Prialé. The price of Aprista support for Lavalle was simple: legalization of the party and permission for it to take part in the election. At first Odría seemed inclined to concede the Apristas' demands, but he finally refused to do so, although he did permit a number of the exiled Aprista leaders to return to Peru.

At the same time, Belaúnde Terry was also seeking the backing of the Apristas. With some reason, he felt that he "deserved" this backing. He had worked with the party in the past, and he was in 1956 closer to them in ideology than either of the other two candidates. Furthermore, he was willing to promise legality to the party if he won. From the point of view of the Apristas, he had two definite handicaps. On the one hand, there was serious doubt that Odría would turn power over to Belaúnde Terry if he won, and the Apristas wanted desperately to regain legal status, and had no intention of making a "heroic gesture." Furthermore, many of the Aprista leaders saw in Belaúnde Terry and the movement which gathered around him the first serious challenge in a quarter of a century to the Aprista party's popularity among the masses.

Prado y Ugarteche was also anxious to get Aprista support. Without it, he stood no chance of winning the presidency again. He was not a popular man; he was the epitome of the oligarchy which had ruled the country for nearly a century and a half. He had not been friendly to the Apristas when he had been president between 1939 and 1945, although just before the 1945 election, to choose his successor, he had legalized the party under the name Partido del Pueblo.

In spite of his past history, Prado y Ugarteche actively sought the backing of the Apristas. For their part, the leaders of the party turned to him about two weeks before the election, when it became clear that Odría and his candidate Lavalle were not going to pay the price necessary to gain Aprista support. After some negotiation, Manuel Prado y Ugarteche agreed to legalize the party as the first act of his new administration, if he were to be elected.

On the basis of this promise, Ramiro Prialé and other leaders of the Aprista party decided to throw their last-minute support to Prado y Ugarteche. They had only about ten days before the election to get word to the party rank and file. They did not succeed in this endeavor in the more remote parts of the country. In some areas, too, there was opposition from party members to the decision to support the former president. However, in the strongest Aprista centers, such as the Lima region, and the northern city of Trujillo, Aprista support for him was overwhelming, sufficient to assure his election.

The Prado y Ugarteche Government

The Prado y Ugarteche administration took office early in July, 1956. It has been a caretaker government, the main task of which has been to maintain a stable government to guarantee the basic democratic freedoms, and to pave the way for the election of 1962, which it is widely believed will be won by the Aprista party, and will inaugurate a new era of democratic reform.

President Prado y Ugarteche honored his promise to push through Congress a law legalizing the Aprista party. Aprista exiles returned, political prisoners were released, and the party began an energetic drive to build its organization throughout the country. The Apristas threw their political support behind the régime, though not forsaking their right to criticize the administration when they felt it to be in error.

Other democratic institutions were restored. Freedom of speech and press were maintained by the Prado y Ugarteche administration. The trade union movement was given full freedom to reorganize, and the Confederación de Trabajadores del Perú was reestablished, under Aprista leadership, with the veteran Aprista textile workers' leader Arturo Sabroso as its secretary general. Most of the urban wage earners, the miners, and even agricultural workers on the sugar plantations were unionized. The reconstituted unions entered into collective bargaining agreements with their employers.

The régime was cautious, and even timid. It sought to avoid any incident which might provoke the army to interfere once again in politics, or to move against the administration. The president hesitated to remove from government service those who were still loyal to Odría, and those who were pro-Communist, even though these people were known to be hostile to the Prado y Ugarteche government and were suspected of sabotaging its policies.

The continuation of President Prado in power until the expiration of his term in 1962 is essential to the future of Peruvian democracy. It is only a matter of time until the revolutionary changes which have occurred in Bolivia since 1952 will take place in neighboring Peru. The maintenance of Prado in office and his handing power over to a democratically elected government pledged to start the reform process is probably the last opportunity for these changes to come peacefully and democratically. A new dictatorship will almost certainly be followed sooner or later by a violent revolution.

The Overthrow of Rojas Pinilla

A little less than a year after the end of the Odría dictatorship in Peru, the tyrannical government of General Gustavo Rojas Pinilla was ousted in Colombia. The overthrow of Rojas Pinilla brought to an end a decade of terror, civil war, and virtual chaos in a country which had once prided itself on its constitutionalism and democracy.

Colombia is a country of two traditional political parties, dating from the early days of the republic, the Conservatives and the Liberals. During the nineteenth century the distinction between them was that the former were supporters of the Church, and the latter were anticlerical. However, during the first three or four decades of the twentieth century, the Liberals dropped most of their anticlericalism and became advocates of a moderate program of social reform.

Although the Liberal governments in power during the 1930's carried out certain economic and social changes, such as the imposition of an income tax, and the enactment of extensive labor legislation, the nature of the economic and social system of Colombia was not fundamentally altered by the Liberal administrations of Presidents Enrique Olaya Herrera, Alfonso López, and Eduardo Santos. The Liberal party, like its opponent, continued to be controlled largely by the country's aristocratic families, which had dominated the republic since its inception.

Popular loyalty to one party or another in Colombia tends to be traditional. This is a case in which the Gilbert and Sullivan ditty:

> ". . . every boy and every gal
>   That's born into the world alive,
> Is either a little Liberal,
>   Or else a little Conservative!"

is apt. In many cases the hatred of a party member for those of the opposite political group tends to be extreme. This fact has added much to political tension in Colombia since the middle 1940's.

A further complication was the fact that important elements of the Conservative party have had little fundamental loyalty to democratic processes. Dr. Laureano Gómez, titular leader of the Conservative party, has been not only an admirer but a personal friend of Spanish dictator Francisco Franco, and was openly and violently in favor of the Axis during World War II.

The intransigent attitude of the Gómez faction of the Conservatives became very important after the election of 1946. This was won by the Conservatives, as a result of a split in the ranks of the Liberal party sparked by a revolt led by Jorge Eliecer Gaitán, who argued that Colombia needed a much more profound reform—including the provision of land for the considerable number of landless peasants—than the successive Liberal governments had provided. He raised a cry against the "Liberal oligarchy," and overnight became an exceedingly popular figure among the city workers, peasants, and young people.

When Gaitán failed to get the Liberal party nomination for president in 1946, he ran anyway, as a dissident Liberal. The result was a victory by Mariano Ospina Pérez, the Conservative nominee, and a representative of the moderate or anti-Gómez faction of the party. Although such was not necessarily the attitude of Ospina Pérez, many Conservatives were determined that, reestablished in power, they would not give up control of the government to the Liberals under any circumstances.

The Death of Gaitán and Its Aftermath

After the Liberal defeat Gaitán, who had gotten considerably more votes than the regular Liberal candidate, was recognized as the undisputed leader of the Liberal party. He was by that time the idol of the masses of Colombia, and particularly of the capital city of Bogotá. He would almost certainly have been elected president of Colombia if he had been alive to take part in the election of 1950.

However, on April 9, 1948, Jorge Gaitán was assassinated. His murderer was lynched by the enraged mob, and as word of Gaitán's death spread through the city, the pro-Liberal populace of Bogotá arose in blind and furious rebellion. Although there was subsequently a good deal of talk about Communist inspiration for this *Bogotazo*, as the revolt came to be known, the Reds had little or no hand in the affair. It was a simple reaction to the sudden assassination of the man who was the hero of the masses of the capital. The enraged mobs burned every building in the center of the city which seemed to have any connection with the Conservative party. At the height of the rebellion, leaders of the Liberal party sought to get President Ospina Pérez to resign, but he refused to do so. Instead, a coalition cabinet equally divided between Conservatives and Liberals was formed.

This attempt to compromise the fratricidal struggle between the Colombian parties failed. Within six months of the *Bogotazo*, the Liberals left the cabinet. Subsequently, the president dissolved Congress and the Council of State, both controlled by the Liberals, and instituted a virtual dictatorship. In an election held in November, 1949, in which the Liberals refused to participate, Laureano Gómez was elected president of the republic.

In the meanwhile, civil war had broken out throughout large

parts of the country. Liberal peasants, persecuted by local Conservative officials, took to the hills and conducted a guerrilla war against the government. With the election of Gómez, an implacable foe of Liberals, the civil strife was intensified. It became difficult and exceedingly risky to travel very far from the country's larger cities.

The Rojas Pinilla Régime

When President Laureano Gómez sought to pave the way for the establishment of a Fascist corporate state by purging from the government all of the members of the Ospina Pérez faction of the Conservatives, including Chief of Staff General Gustavo Rojas Pinilla, the army, led by Rojas, deposed the president. The seizure of power by General Rojas Pinilla was welcomed by the Liberal party as well as by the Ospina Pérez faction of the Conservatives. The new president offered a general amnesty to all who had been in arms against the Gómez administration and called upon all parties and factions to work for a national reconciliation. He promised to call elections quickly to reestablish a democratic régime.

For about a year, President Rojas Pinilla continued to maintain his popularity among all political factions except the Gómez Conservatives. In June, 1954, the first serious crisis occurred. A demonstration of students of the National University in Bogotá was attacked by police and soldiers, and several students were killed. A few weeks later, in conformity with a program he had announced for amending the Constitution, he named a large number of additional members to a Constituent Assembly which had been hand-picked by Laureano Gómez. In making his choices of people to represent the Liberals, Rojas Pinilla ignored many of those nominated by the Liberal National Executive so that most of those whom he named as Liberal members refused to serve in the Assembly.

After this break with the Liberal party, Rojas Pinilla became increasingly arbitrary. He established a government-subsidized newspaper, while at the same time suppressing the internationally famous Liberal dailies *El Tiempo* and *El Espectador*. He sought to set up a government-controlled labor movement. A social welfare organization headed by the President's wife, and patterned after the Eva Perón Foundation in Argentina was established. Meanwhile, the members of the armed forces, whose representatives the Rojas Pinilla government claimed to be, became increasingly arrogant in their relations with the civilians.

The President, though, was an avid speechmaker, and spent much of his time touring the country, addressing crowds of workers, peasants, and other representatives of the common folk. In many of these discourses, Rojas Pinilla talked vaguely of the need for profound social and economic reform in Colombia. Although he took few steps toward putting any of these ideas into practice, the president did carry on a good deal of agitation which was to have important consequences.

This aspect of the Rojas Pinilla leadership won it the backing of somewhat unexpected elements. A group of former associates of Jorge Eliecer Gaitán, including his widow, organized into the Independent Liberal party, and backed the Rojas Pinilla régime. So did the Popular Socialist party, the country's small but active democratic Socialist party.

End of the Rojas Pinilla Administration

The increasingly dictatorial nature of the Rojas administration brought about a reconciliation between the leaders of the country's two major political parties. The Liberals, now led by ex-President Alberto Lleras Camargo, who had returned from a ten-year period of service as head of the Organization of American States to take over the reins of his party, entered into negotiations with the inveterate enemy of the Liberals, Laureano

Gómez. He twice visited Spain, where Gómez was in exile, and worked out a program of cooperation between the two parties for the overthrow of Rojas Pinilla and for the subsequent reestablishment of constitutional government. By the middle of 1956 the two parties were working closely together against the dictatorship.

The struggle between the two traditional parties and the government came to a climax early in 1957. By that time the dictatorship had fallen afoul of the Church, partly because of the government's attempt to centralize all social welfare activities in its own hands, partly because of the Rojas régime's attempt to capture or destroy the Church-supported labor movement, the Unión de Trabajadores de Colombia. The hierarchy of the Colombian Church directed several pastoral letters of warning and admonishment to the Rojas government in 1956 and early 1957.

During the first days of May, 1957, rioting broke out on a large scale in Bogotá and other important cities. The university students played a leading role in this movement, which developed into a virtual insurrection, but there was little doubt that the leadership of the two parties was behind the whole thing.

Rojas temporized with the rioters, which was probably his downfall. Some of his advisers urged him to declare a state of siege and simultaneously announce the inauguration of a vast reform program, thus appealing to the rank and file of the citizenry over the heads of the Liberal and Conservative party leaders. This he failed to do, and finally, on May 9, the principal leaders of the armed forces insisted that Rojas Pinilla resign and seek refuge abroad. A military junta, consisting of the chief officers of the army, navy, and air force, took over from the resigning dictator.

The Restoration of Constitutional Government

The junta which ousted Rojas Pinilla announced its intention to lead the country back to constitutional government. It did so along lines agreed upon by the leaders of the two major parties. They had drawn up an accord whereby for a period of twelve years the presidency would rotate between members of the Conservative and Liberal parties, with the first chief executive being a Conservative. At the same time, they agreed that membership of Congress, as well as provincial governorships and other key posts would be divided equally between the two parties.

This agreement was formulated in an amendment to the national constitution, which was submitted to the voters for approval and received their support. Elections were then called for president and congress. The whole arrangement was threatened when the Conservative party was unable to agree on who from its ranks should become president under the new system. The problem was finally resolved by extending the period of political truce to sixteen years and agreeing that Liberal leader Alberto Lleras Camargo would be the first chief executive backed by both parties.

The elections early in 1958 were the first opportunity the Colombian people had had in twelve years to indicate which of the two parties they favored. Although an equal number of congressmen were elected for each party, as had been agreed, the Liberals gained half again as many votes as did the Conservatives.

The Future of Democracy in Colombia

On May 4, 1958, Alberto Lleras Camargo was inaugurated as president, thus restoring constitutional and civilian government, but the fate of democracy in Colombia still hung in the balance. All political groups recognized that the compromise reached between the two major parties was a peculiar one, and that it was precarious and would need a great deal of tolerance and tact on both sides in order to make it work. Furthermore, the compromise itself was in a real sense a negation of democracy, since the voters would have little to say about who would be chief executive or would sit in congress for a period of sixteen years.

At best, it could be regarded only as an arrangement to pave the way for the restoration of a really democratic government.

Colombia's crisis had had two fundamental causes: the failure of the old parties to bring about popular participation in the process of government; and the unwillingness of the Conservatives to give up power once they had achieved it. Although the latter problem seemed to have been at least partially resolved by the Great Compromise, the former was far from resolution even after the inauguration of Lleras Camargo.

There is little doubt that the uncompromising attitude of many Conservative leaders, particularly Gómez and his associates, toward the Liberals and their determination to hold on to power at any price, was one of the principal causes of the troubles of the 1948-1958 period. The Conservative régimes violently persecuted Liberals, tens of thousands of whom were murdered by police and soldiers. They made it impossible for the Liberals to play the role of a loyal opposition, because they would not concede the possibility of the Liberals once again assuming power if the electorate so decided. However, the arrangement between Lleras Camargo and Gómez seemed to indicate that the Conservatives had realized the error of their ways and to have concluded that Liberal rule was to be preferred to military dictatorship.

The more fundamental problem of social reform still faced the new administration. The quick rise of Jorge Eliecer Gaitán in the early 1940's had indicated a fundamental discontent among large masses of the people, and a belief that the traditional oligarchy which dominated both parties was unwilling to bring about changes which were long overdue. The experience of the Rojas Pinilla government had intensified rather than lessened this discontent.

No one is more aware than President Lleras Camargo of the gravity of this problem. The great question facing him and all sincere democrats in Colombia is whether or not they will be able to push through needed reforms, including a redistribution of the land, in time to head off the development of a totalitarian movement which would put an end to all possibility of democratic life in the republic. It is highly significant that in the months following the fall of Rojas Pinilla the Communists "came back" politically with a force which they had not had since the 1945-1946 period, when Gaitán had virtually destroyed the Communist party by taking away from it almost all of those workers, young people, and peasants who had been the basis for its growth in the late 1930's and early 1940's.

The Establishment of Democratic Government in Honduras

One of the brightest spots in Latin America in recent years has been the Central American republic of Honduras. This small country had never really enjoyed a democratic government, and during the 1930's and most of the 1940's had suffered one of the hemisphere's most severe dictatorships, that of General Tiburcio Carías Andino. However, between 1948 and 1957 Honduras went through a painful process of evolution, which culminated late in 1957 in the inauguration of a democratically elected civilian president.

Honduras has been one of the most backward and isolated of the Latin American republics. Industry is incipient, and only along the northern coast where the United Fruit Company and the Standard Fruit and Steamship Company established large banana empires has the country any appreciable contact with modern economic and social problems. Politically, Honduras has rotated among a long series of dictatorships, generally led by uncouth and self-made military men. The Liberal and National (Conservative) party labels have been all but meaningless until very recent years.

Early in the 1930's General Tiburcio Carías Andino seized power. His dictatorship was brutal, effective, and all-encompassing. His Partido Nacional was the only political organization allowed to function, and leaders of the Liberal party were jailed, executed, shipped off into exile, or forced to lapse into silence and inactivity.

In 1948, General Carías Andino decided to retire from the presidency. He placed in the office Dr. Juan Manuel Gálvez, a civilian. Dr. Gálvez was a very different type of man from his predecessor. Aware of modern currents of political thought, he sought slowly to put an end to the dictatorship which he had inherited, while at the same time launching a modest program of economic development and social change.

Gálvez allowed many of the political exiles to return. He permitted the Liberal party to reorganize and to conduct open political activities and gave a considerable degree of freedom of press. As a result, there was an inevitable break between Gálvez and Carías, with the consequence that the Gálvez supporters organized a third political party, the Movimiento Reformista.

The Liberals, in the meanwhile, had emerged as a new kind of party, insofar as Honduras was concerned. The party had a new and young leadership of high-caliber professional people. It took a position as the spokesman for the emerging trade union movement, which had suddenly appeared in May, 1954, as the result of a general strike in the banana fields. It urged a wide program of economic development, the enactment of a labor code, and other measures which would tend to put Honduras abreast of the other Latin American nations.

President Gálvez' term of office expired in 1954 and late that year there was a general election, with three presidential candidates, representing the Nacional, Reformista, and Liberal parties. Although it was widely believed that the Liberal candidate, Dr. José Ramón Villeda Morales had won, the official figures of the government indicated that none of the three nominees had received 51 per cent of the vote as required by the constitution. The election was thrown into the national congress, which was also unable to select the winner. As a result, Acting President Julio Lozano Díaz, who had taken over when President Gálvez resigned because of ill health, declared a "constitutional dictator-ship" on December 6, 1954, dissolving Congress and promising to hold elections within a year.

In spite of his promises, President Lozano Díaz sought to con-tinue in office. He tightened the reins of his dictatorship, arresting many of his political opponents, particularly among the Liberals, and forcing others, including Villeda Morales, into exile. On October 21, 1956, Lozano Díaz was overthrown by an army coup, and a three-man military junta took over, pledged once again to call elections and to install a democratic civilian régime.

The junta was as good as its word. Political freedom was re-established, exiles returned, prisoners were released, and Dr. Villeda Morales was named Ambassador to Washington. Late in 1957 general elections were held for a constituent assembly, elec-tions which were won by the Liberals. The assembly wrote a new constitution, and as its final act elected Dr. José Ramón Villeda Morales president of the republic. He took office in December, 1957.

The fate of democracy in Honduras is still precarious. The opponents of the Liberals have not yet given up the idea that the government can and should be overthrown by *coup d'état*. At the same time, the president is highly dependent on the good will of the armed forces in order to stay in power. Nevertheless, for the first time in several decades the country has a constitutionally elected régime. The Liberals are aware of the social and economic problems facing the republic and are anxious to come to grips with them. Their success in doing so will go far to determine whether or not a democratic administration will continue in that little republic.

Summary and Conclusion

Democracy is not yet firmly entrenched in Peru, Colombia, or Honduras, but events of recent years have given it a chance in all three of these republics. Its future in each of them depends on the ability of the democratic groups now in control to meet the social and economic problems which face their respective republics, thus building up the prestige of democratic ideas and sowing the conviction among the masses of the people that they can best attain their objectives through the democratic process.

CHAPTER SEVEN

SOME RECENT
DEMOCRATIC VICTORIES
PART THREE:
THE END OF THE
PÉREZ JIMÉNEZ RÉGIME

One of the most brutal and vicious dictatorships which has existed in Latin America in recent years was that of General Marcos Pérez Jiménez in Venezuela. Perhaps its suppression of opposition, its imprisonment, torture, and murder of opponents have been surpassed only by the tyranny of Generalissimo Rafael Trujillo Molina in the Dominican Republic. Yet its downfall is testimony to the ability of the new political forces in Latin America to carry on a long struggle against dictatorship and come through this struggle with victory.

The Antecedents of the Pérez Jiménez Dictatorship

Virtually since independence Venezuela has been governed by a series of military dictatorships. Of these, the rule of General Juan Vicente Gómez, who gained unhappy renown as "The Tyrant of the Andes," became world famous. During his period

111

of control, which lasted from 1909 until 1935, the exploitation of oil began in the region of Lake Maracaibo. With the help of revenues from the petroleum industry, Gómez succeeded in turning virtually all property worth owning in Venezuela into his personal possession.

The Gómez régime was absolutist in its scope. There was no pretense of legal opposition to political activity during his rule. The press was servile, and thousands of students, professional men, army officers, and workers were jailed, tortured, driven into exile, or even murdered. In spite of the brutality, there existed an underground ferment which burst loose after Gómez disappeared.

The Tyrant of the Andes died in bed, in his sleep, in December, 1935. His position as president was taken by his son-in-law and Minister of War, General Eleázar López Contreras. The new chief executive relaxed the rigidity of the dictatorship and for almost a year allowed the development of political activity, the growth of a labor movement, and a considerable degree of freedom of press, speech, and assembly. Then this opposition activity began to grow beyond the bounds which López Contreras felt he could control, and he cracked down on his opponents, exiling most of them and driving others into hiding.

Two important political groups developed during the López Contreras dictatorship. One of these was the Partido Nacional Democrático, a left-wing democratic group, advocating trade union organization, labor legislation, low-cost housing, agrarian reform, and a fundamental change in the government's petroleum policy. The other was the Partido Comunista, the Venezuelan affiliate of the Communist International. These two groups competed for control of the incipient labor movement, and sought to gain support among the general populace.

General López Contreras' administration ended in 1941. His hand-picked nominee, General Isaías Medina Angarita, succeeded him in the presidency. General Medina Angarita's régime ended many of the aspects of the dictatorship. All exiles were allowed to return, the Partido Nacional Democrático, which reorganized as Acción Democrática, and the Partido Comunista were allowed to function legally, the latter becoming a close collaborator with the Medina Angarita administration. The labor movement was encouraged; virtually complete freedom of press and speech and party organization was allowed.

In spite of his relaxation of the dictatorship, General Medina Angarita would not agree to permit a free election of his successor in 1945. Acción Democrática tried to get him to do so, and when they failed in that, the AD leaders urged the president to agree on a joint nominee to be supported by both the administration and the opposition. This proposal, too, the president rejected.

Meanwhile, a group of young army officers were plotting a revolt against the government. Some of them were motivated by a desire to see the establishment of a full democracy. Others were moved by resentment at the fact that a considerable number of old generals were blocking the road to promotion. Most of these junior officers were men with more or less advanced technical training, while the generals were self-taught practical soldiers, who had reached their positions during the civil wars of the early years of the century and by service to the Gómez dictatorship.

The plotting captains and majors approached Acción Democrática, urging its leaders to cooperate in a revolt. After exhausting all possibility of negotiation with Medina Angarita concerning the presidential election, the Acción Democrática leaders finally agreed, fearing that if they did not do so, the rebels might reestablish the Gómez type of administration. The upshot was the revolution of October 28, 1945.

The régime established by the rebels was dominated by Acción Democrática. A nine-man junta, presided over by Acción Democrática chief Rómulo Betancourt, was established. It consisted of six members of the party, one independent civilian, Dr. Edmundo Fernández, and two military men, Major Carlos Delgado Chalbaud and Captain Mario Vargas. It remained in power for two years, during which it presided over two elections, one for a constituent assembly, and the second for president, congress, and all the state legislatures. Rómulo Gallegos, one of Latin America's most famous novelists and the nominee of the Acción Democrática, was elected president and took office early in 1948. However, he stayed in office only until November 24, 1948, when he was ousted by a military *coup d'état*.

During the three years in which Acción Democrática was in power, it carried out an extensive program of economic, social, and political reform. It worked out the famous 50-50 arrangement whereby the oil companies' profits were divided evenly between the firms and the government. The increased revenues coming to the government were spent partly on a program to diversify the economy by extending agricultural production through irrigation and settling of colonies of Venezuelans and European immigrants on government land, as well as by encouraging industrialization through extensive government loans to entrepreneurs. Other funds were spent on a large housing program, on a dramatic increase in schools, student enrollment, and teacher training, and an extension of the country's social security system.

The Acción Democrática administration was the most democratic government Venezuela had ever known. Freedom of speech and organization were generally respected. Several new political parties appeared, the most important being the Social Catholic (COPEI) party and the Unión Republicana Democrática, a party similar to Acción Democrática in ideology, but separated by certain personal objections of URD chiefs to Betancourt and other leaders of Acción Democrática. There was virtually complete freedom of the press. Trade unions grew spectacularly in number, and collective bargaining became the rule in Venezuelan labor relations.

The success of the Acción Democrática government imperiled the army's traditional role as the dominant factor in Venezuelan politics. Certain military leaders resented the growing power of the political parties, trade unions, and other civilian organizations which occurred after 1945. Plots were constant throughout the 1945-1948 period, but until November of the latter year they were overcome with more or less difficulty by the AD régime.

Early in November, 1948, a group of army officers led by Colonel Marcos Pérez Jiménez presented an ultimatum to President Rómulo Gallegos, demanding the organization of a cabinet with a majority of military men, a curbing of the activities of the Acción Democrática party and of the trade unions, and other items. President Gallegos temporized, did not submit to the ultimatum, but did not arrest the offending officers. Finally, on November 24, the rebels struck.

The Junta

The rebel officers established a three-man military junta to run the government, headed by Colonel Carlos Delgado Chalbaud, who had been President Gallegos' Minister of War and had only joined the *coup d'état* at the last moment. The other members were Colonels Marcos Pérez Jiménez and Federico Llovera Páez.

The junta government reversed most of the policies pursued by the Acción Democrática government. Acción Democrática itself was outlawed, while other parties were seriously hampered in their public activities. Large numbers of AD leaders were jailed, and some were killed. The economic development program launched by Acción Democrática was allowed to lapse, and the expansion of educational facilities was brought to a halt. The government spent its large oil revenues on the military and on spectacular public works programs, particularly in Caracas. Hundreds of millions of dollars were stolen by members of the régime, and much of this loot was shipped abroad.

In 1950 the president of the junta, Colonel Delgado Chalbaud, was kidnaped and murdered. Colonel Peréz Jiménez became the dominant figure in the government, while a civilian, German Suarez Flamerich, was named to take Delgado Chalbaud's place in the junta.

The junta called elections for December, 1952. Acción Democrática was not allowed to participate, but the Unión Republicana Democrática and COPEI were allowed to name candidates, while the nominees of the government ran on a list called the Frente Electoral Independiente (FEI). At the last moment outlawed Acción Democrática threw its support behind the URD. Much to the surprise of the members of the junta, the URD ran far ahead when election returns began coming in. Next was COPEI, and the FEI received only about 20 per cent of the total vote.

The defeat in the election presented the junta with a crisis. It was met by a suspension of the counting of the ballots, and then the announcement by Colonel Pérez Jiménez that he was assuming power as provisional president. A few days later, the new president announced that the FEI had won an "overwhelming victory" in the elections. The "victorious" candidates met as a constituent assembly in January, 1953, wrote a new constitution, and then elected Pérez Jiménez as "constitutional president."

The Pérez Jiménez Régime

The Pérez Jiménez administration was more ferocious than the junta had been. The Unión Republicana Democrática was outlawed as the AD had previously been. The third party, the Christian Social COPEI, was not outlawed, but it was not allowed to carry on any public activities, its leaders were frequently arrested, some of them were exiled, and a few were killed. The government set up a concentration camp in the wilds of the Orinoco River Valley, where political prisoners of all classes and political parties were sent. Many fell sick of dysentery and other diseases; others died as a result of the inhuman treatment they received.

The persecution of the enemies of the dictatorship was in the hands of the secret police, the notorious Seguridad Nacional. Headed by the infamous Pedro Estrada, this organization could probably have given lessons to the Nazi Gestapo or the Soviet GPU. It had an all-encompassing spy system, which kept as close track on the officer corps of the armed forces as it did on the civilians. The Seguridad Nacional employed a choice group of torturers who developed exquisite techniques for destroying the wills and bodies of their victims. Those submitted to its tortures numbered in the thousands and no one, perhaps not even the dictator himself, was free from the surveillance of the Seguridad Nacional.

While tirelessly persecuting the democratic parties, the Pérez Jiménez government tolerated and even encouraged Communist penetration of the labor movement. Until shortly before the fall of the dictatorship, one faction of the Communists—the so-called Black Communists—were permitted to maintain regional trade union federations in Caracas and other centers, which were affiliated with the Communist international labor movement. Leaders of these groups were allowed to go back and forth between Venezuela and the Iron Curtain.

In addition to being arbitrary, the Pérez Jiménez clique was extremely corrupt. *The New York Times* reported soon after the fall of Pérez Jiménez that he himself had accumulated a fortune of some $235,000,000. Other members of the favored coterie undoubtedly stole other hundreds of millions of dollars. Anyone doing business in Venezuela during these years was forced to pay illegal tribute to "collectors." Not even the poorest citizens were safe from the exactions of these gentlemen.

The dictatorship had no interest in the kind of economic

development program which Acción Democrática had launched. Agriculture was virtually ignored. Although the prosperity brought about by the tremendous expansion of the country's petroleum industry during those years brought with it the development of a number of new industries, little of this was attributable to Pérez Jiménez. Although the AD government had virtually concluded negotiations for the establishment of an iron and steel plant in the eastern part of the country, it took the AD's successors seven years finally to get this plant under way.

The oil policy of the dictatorship was a reversal of the position which had been held by all governments since 1943. Since that time it had been the official policy not to grant any new concessions to private oil companies, but to keep the remaining oil reserves of the nation as the possible basis for development of a national petroleum industry, when the opportunity to establish such an enterprise seemed ripe.

The Pérez Jiménez dictatorship, eager to get more opportunities to enrich its members, decided to grant new concessions. It did so in 1955 and 1956. Most of these were given to a firm known as Venezuelan Leaseholds, composed of people who were not oilmen. *The New York Times* noted on September 14, 1956, that this company "has been the object of considerable speculation." It sold its concessions to operating oil firms. This oil policy outraged virtually all patriotic Venezuelans.

The Downfall of Pérez Jiménez

From November 24, 1948, the Venezuelan dictatorship was faced with bitter opposition, participated in by members of all political parties, but the burden of the struggle was carried by Acción Democrática. The AD had been able throughout the whole period of the tyranny to maintain an active underground. Several of the leaders of this opposition, including national secretaries of the party Leonardo Ruiz Pineda and Alberto

Carnevali, were killed by the police. Thousands of other Acción Democrática leaders were jailed, sent to the Guasina concentration camp, tortured, murdered, exiled.

The AD underground maintained its own press and gave leadership to rank-and-file members of many of the unions, even though their ostensible officials were government puppets. During the 1952 election, AD support for the Unión Republicana Democrática was crucial in the URD's spectacular "victory," the victory of which it was robbed by Pérez Jiménez.

After the 1952 election, the URD also joined the underground. Although the Catholic Social Party, COPEI, was ostensibly legal, it too was forced to adopt underground methods in fighting against Pérez Jiménez after 1952.

During 1957 the continued struggle of the political parties against the government began to gain new recruits. On May 1, the majority of the bishops of the Catholic Church in Venezuela, headed by the Archbishop of Caracas, issued a pastoral letter in which they attacked the oppression of the government and severely criticized its retrograde social policies.

The year 1957 was sure in any case to be a year of crisis for Pérez Jiménez. His term of office came to an end early in 1958 and it would be necessary for him to do something about the succession, or more specifically, find some way to have himself reelected. After postponing a decision until two months before the time for the election in December, 1957, he finally selected a unique method of securing his objective. Instead of running the risk of even a rigged election, the dictator decided to have a "plebiscite." The voters were given the chance only to vote "yes" or "no" on the reelection of Pérez Jiménez. No provision was made in the law for what was to occur should a "no" vote predominate. But there was no chance of that. All government employees were forced to show their "no" cards when they came to work on the day after the election. Employees of some private firms were given the same orders. Large numbers of

those opposed did not even bother to vote, since the result wa
known before the election was even held.

Although Pérez Jiménez was "reelected" early in December
less than a month and a half later he was out of office. The
plebiscite proved to be the one step too many taken by the
dictator. It aroused the indignation of many citizens who had
not bothered their heads about politics previously. It also held
him up to pitiless ridicule by the opposition. Those who were
outraged by the plebiscite included many members of the armed
forces. The most significant result of the plebiscite was the
fact that the people had suddenly lost their fear of the dictator
and were willing to go out in the streets and struggle openly
against him.

The first blow came on January 1st, when the air force—the
strongest in Latin America—arose in revolt. Although this up
rising was suppressed after only a few hours and most of the
air force flew off to refuge in neighboring Colombia, this prove
to be only the beginning of the end for Pérez Jiménez. Civilia
disturbances in the streets of Caracas and other major cities gre
in intensity after January 1st. Meanwhile, leading military off
cers forced Pérez Jiménez to exile Pedro Estrada, head of th
Seguridad Nacional, and Minister of the Interior Valenilla Lan
to the Dominican Republic.

Conditions grew increasingly chaotic. The struggle against th
tyrant was led by the so-called Junta Patriótica, composed o
two representatives each from the Acción Democrática, COPE
Unión Republicana Democrática, and Communist parties. Th
Junta called a general strike on January 22, a walkout which wa
supported by virtually all employers and was launched by th
ringing of church bells throughout the country.

The general strike was accompanied by street fighting, an
finally, on January 23rd, the top leaders of the armed forc
refused to support Pérez Jiménez any further. They demande

his immediate resignation, and packed him off on a plane for the Dominican Republic.

The Restoration of Democratic Government

A new government junta was established to take Pérez Jiménez' place. It consisted of one representative each of the army, navy, and air force, in addition to two civilians, chosen from among the country's most distinguished and wealthiest businessmen. Its president was Admiral Wolfgang Larrazábal. It immediately announced that its job was to restore democratic constitutional government to Venezuela.

Once again exiles returned, political prisoners were released, and full freedom of speech, press, assembly, and organization was established. The three major democratic parties, Acción Democrática, the Christian Social COPEI and the URD, reorganized their ranks and it soon became clear that they represented the great majority of the people of the nation. The Communists also returned to legal activity and at least one new party appeared upon the scene. This was a group known as Integración Republicana, which was the spokesman for certain business and professional people who did not feel at home in any of the older parties.

The provisional government had serious problems to face. The dictatorship had left over $200,000,000 in debts, largely in the form of IOU's and unpaid bills to building contractors and suppliers. The government agreed to recognize all these debts and attempt to pay them off as soon as possible. However, the financial position was weakened by the recession in the United States, and moves by that country to restrict importation of Venezuelan oil. This resulted in a decline of about 10 per cent in the amount of oil shipped to the U.S., with a consequent fall in the government's income from petroleum.

The junta was faced with several attempts by partisans of the dictatorship to overthrow it by a *coup d'état*. Two insurrectional attempts occurred, one in July and the other in September, 1958. They both failed in the face of the loyalty of the majority of the armed forces, and of a general strike by the reorganized labor movement, backed by the country's employers' organizations, which declared a general lockout both times. This unity of workers and employers in defense of an administration which was reestablishing democracy was a new phenomenon in Venezuelan politics and augured well for the future of democracy in the country.

The civilians attempted to maintain a united front to prevent any effort by military elements to reinstitute a dictatorship. After a short period in which the leaders of Acción Democrática, URD, COPEI, and the Communists consulted together regularly, the united front of parties was reorganized and the Communists were dropped. However, the three democratic parties worked closely together throughout the period of the provisional government.

The principal job of the junta was to hold elections and allow the people to decide whom they wanted to govern. It proceeded swiftly with this job. By June, 1958, an electoral statute had been adopted, and a few weeks later there was a nation-wide registration of voters. However, there was a long period of uncertainty concerning who would be the candidates for president. At first an attempt was made to have the three democratic parties agree on a single candidate. When all such negotiations failed, each of the three parties put up its own nominee.

The election of December, 1958, was hotly contested. Acción Democrática named its founder and president, Rómulo Betancourt. COPEI nominated its founder and most important leader, Dr. Rafael Caldera. URD put up Admiral Larrazábal, who had guided the government junta through its first difficult months. The smaller parties backed one or the other of these nominees— Integración Republicana supporting Caldera and the Communists backing Larrazábal.

The three candidates campaigned vigorously throughout the country. There were few incidents during the campaign, and the election itself went off quietly. When the votes had been counted they showed that Rómulo Betancourt had been elected, with approximately 49 per cent of the vote. Admiral Larrazábal had come in second, winning a smashing victory in the city of Caracas, though losing in the interior of the country. Dr. Caldera came in third.

On February 13, 1959, Rómulo Betancourt was inaugurated as constitutional president of the republic in a very impressive ceremony held in the chambers of the Senate. As the result of an agreement among the democratic parties, President Betancourt named a coalition cabinet with representatives of all three parties as well as a number of independent technicians. There was a wide area of agreement among the parties on a program which in essence was a continuation of that which Betancourt had launched when he was president between 1945 and 1948. All parties supported agrarian reform, the establishment of a national oil firm, the encouragement of industrialization, the stimulation of agricultural production, the extension of educational and social services. There was also universal accord among the leaders of the three parties on the need for presenting a united front to the military, to consolidate the democratic system which had been rewon at such a tremendous cost in suffering and in lives.

Summary and Conclusion

The struggle for democracy in Venezuela has been particularly bitter and prolonged. However, it is notable because of the tenacity with which the leaders and members of the democratic political parties have persisted in their efforts to oust dictatorships, even when the possibility of success seemed dimmest. It also is notable for the mature attitude which the party leaders demonstrated after the fall of Pérez Jiménez and their determination to maintain a civilian united front to prevent the return of a military tyranny. Finally, the degree to which nonpolitical civilian groups, such as the trade union movement and the organized employers, have seconded the attitude of the political party leaders is equally worthy of comment.

Venezuelan democracy will depend largely on the Betancourt government's ability to carry out its program of social change and economic development. As this is being written (June, 1960), the government has just launched an all-out agrarian reform, and the president has presented a program of economic development to cover the last four years of his administration. These events and the success of the new incumbents in thwarting all efforts of disaffected military men to overthrow them, gives reason for moderate optimism, though democracy is still in danger in Venezuela.

CHAPTER EIGHT

SOME RECENT

DEMOCRATIC VICTORIES

PART FOUR:

THE FALL OF BATISTA

The struggle to overthrow the dictatorship of General Fulgencio Batista Zaldívar began on the day he seized power, March 10, 1952. From that date until he resigned and fled to seek "refuge" in the Dominican Republic of Generalissimo Rafael Trujillo Molina on January 1, 1959, the Cuban people were unwilling to accept the usurper as the legitimate ruler of the island republic.

The Background of the Batista Dictatorship

This was not the first time that Batista had been in power. He had first seized control of Cuba's affairs in September, 1933, when he organized a revolt among noncommissioned army officers which overthrew the weak provisional president then in power and resulted in Batista being suddenly promoted from sergeant to colonel and becoming chief of staff.

In this first coup, the sergeant worked closely with a group of faculty members and students of the University of Havana, led by Dr. Ramón Grau San Martín of the Medical School, who became provisional president. However, within three months, ex-Sergeant Batista overthrew his erstwhile partner, when the United States Department of State refused to recognize Dr. Grau San Martín's government.

During the six years between 1934 and 1940 Colonel Batista made and unmade several presidents. But by the latter year he had tired of merely being the power behind the throne and wanted to sit on it himself. After presiding over elections to choose a constitutional assembly which wrote one of the most democratic and progressive constitutions of contemporary Latin America, the colonel was chosen president of the republic in reasonably honest elections.

During his four years in the presidency Batista followed a democratic pattern of allowing freedom of speech, press, and organization. At the end of his constitutional period, he called elections, which were won by Dr. Ramón Grau San Martín, who was by that time Batista's bitterest enemy. Batista won a unique niche for himself in Cuban and Latin American history, when he allowed Dr. Grau San Martín to take over the reins of power in the middle of 1944.

For the next eight years the government was in the hands of two democratic presidents—Ramón Grau San Martín and Carlos Prío Socorrás—members of the Partido Revolucionario Cubano (Auténtico), generally known as the Auténticos. Although these administrations were corrupt and law enforcement tended to be lax, there probably existed the widest degree of personal and political freedom which the island has ever known.

The Coup of March 10, 1952

On June 1, 1952, another presidential election was scheduled. The Auténtico party named Carlos Hevía, a distinguished engineer, as its candidate. The Ortodoxo party, which had been established by dissident Auténticos who were offended by the corruption of the Grau San Martín and Prío Socorrás administrations, nominated Dr. Roberto Agramonte, a professor of sociology at the University of Havana. General Batista was named by his own Partido de Acción Popular.

There was a great deal of controversy concerning who would win the 1952 election. The odds seemed to favor Dr. Agramonte, though the Auténticos were hopeful that they would be victorious. The one thing which was universally agreed was that General Batista didn't stand a chance.

Faced with the impossibility of once again becoming president by the choice of the people of Cuba, Batista took an action which not only betrayed his country, but also destroyed his position in Cuban history. With the aid of a small group of junior officers of the Camp Columbia garrison just outside Havana, Batista seized power by force on March 10, 1952.

Batista tried to give his rule an aura of legitimacy. He planned to have one of his close collaborators elected president of the Senate, and then succeed constitutionally to the presidency, with the excuse that the deposed president, Carlos Prío Socorrás, had left the country "without permission of Congress" as was required by the constitution. He hoped that this puppet régime would then be able to do enough for enough people to make its real chief, Batista, popular. He would then be able to get elected to the presidency in honest elections.

However, Batista's "constitutional" plans were thwarted when the president of the Senate, Dr. Antonio Varona, refused to resign from his post; instead, he summoned a meeting of Congress for the purpose of legally barring Batista or anyone of his choice from the presidency. The senators and representatives gathered in front of the Capitol, but they were barred from entering it by members of the armed forces. Batista then declared himself "Chief of State," dissolved Congress, and continued in office until shortly before "elections," which he finally called at the end of 1954.

Opposition to Batista

Those opposed to the dictatorship began an underground struggle almost immediately. The lead was taken by university students and elements in the trade unions. On March 10, 1952, the students had asked President Prío for arms to protect his administration against Batista's coup, but he did not cooperate. The students continued to be strongly opposed to Batista from the time he arbitrarily seized power until he was overthrown almost seven years later.

The leaders of the Confederación de Trabajadores de Cuba called a general strike on the morning of Batista's coup. It was unsuccessful, because by the time it was called, Batista already had control of the radio and television stations, and orders for the strike could not be transmitted to rank-and-file trade unionists. The Confederation leaders subsequently made a truce with Batista. During the latter years of his administration, the top labor leaders were forced more and more into a position of supporting the dictator, and the Confederation became, along with the army, one of the two principal supports of the dictatorship. In spite of this growing friendliness toward Batista of the top figures in the Confederation, a few of its principal leaders and many secondary figures in the labor movement entered into underground activity to overthrow the dictator.

Underground organization was supplemented by attempts at forceful action against the dictatorship. On July 26, 1953, a group of students and recent university graduates, led by Fidel Castro, chairman of the Ortodoxo party in Havana Province, made a futile attempt to seize the Moncada Barracks in Santiago de Cuba, the nation's second largest city. It was defeated and those attackers who were not killed were captured and sentenced to long terms in prison. However, they were freed during the following year when Batista declared an amnesty in an attempt to calm popular opposition.

During the next two years, from 1954 to the end of 1956, the violence against Batista was largely confined to individual attempts against leading figures in the administration. Meanwhile, the "election" called by Batista in November, 1954, in which he became "constitutional" president, did not serve to convince the Cuban people that Batista was their legitimate ruler. His only opponent, Dr. Grau San Martín, withdrew before polling day, claiming that the election was rigged by the government.

Military Insurrection

In December, 1956, a new and successful attempt was made to launch a military uprising against the dictator. Fidel Castro, who had led the 1953 attack on the Moncada Barracks, led a landing of Cuban exiles from Mexico at the eastern end of the island in Oriente Province. Only twelve of the eighty invaders survived the landing, but they were able to reach the Sierra Maestra Mountains, where they formed the nucleus of a guerrilla army which by the end of 1958 was to become a force of 10,000 men.

At first, Batista tried to claim that Fidel Castro and all of his followers had been killed, but this myth was exploded when *New York Times* correspondent Herbert Matthews went to the Sierra Maestra, interviewed Castro, and took pictures of him and some of his followers. From then on everyone in Cuba knew that there was an active military insurrection afoot against Batista.

About six months after the launching of the insurrection in the Sierra Maestra, a second front was opened against Batista in the central province of Las Villas. This front was opened by leaders and members of the Revolutionary Student Directorate, established by the University Students Federation as its illegal arm to struggle against the dictatorship.

The government used all possible resources to stamp out the

rebellion. Mass deportations of peasants from the areas affected by the uprising resulted only in turning many of those deported into active guerrilla fighters. Napalm bombs were used in attempts to burn out the areas held by the rebels. Close watch was kept along the extensive coast line of the republic to prevent the landing of new arms supplies for the rebels. In spite of these efforts, about one shipment in every three sent to the insurrectionists from neighboring countries reached its destination. Large quantities of arms were also seized from Batista's own soldiers.

Thus the rebellion slowly gathered force. The 40,000-man army of Batista, his powerful air force, and his navy were inadequate to the task of suppressing the revolt, which got extensive support from the people of the cities in the form of money, supplies, and new recruits. Slowly the rebel forces grew into a full-scale guerrilla army, and by the last half of 1958 the revolutionaries were ready to break out of their mountain fastnesses to offer open battle to the armed forces of the government.

The Underground Front Against the Dictatorship

The military insurrection was supplemented by an ever-growing civilian underground network in Havana and other cities and towns. Indeed, there were several underground organizations. The 26th of July Movement of Fidel Castro was the largest of these. It built up five-man groups in a large number of trade unions throughout the country, and other cells of the movement were established among students, professional people, and other social groups.

The 26th of July Movement, both in the underground and in the Sierra Maestra Mountains, was heterogeneous. It absorbed most of the elements which had formerly belonged to the Partido Ortodoxo, of which Castro himself had been a member and local leader. It also drew many recruits from Catholic groups such as the Young Catholic Workers organization. Many of the guerrilla fighters were peasants who resented reprisals taken against them by the government, but were politically untutored. During the last months of the guerrilla fighting some Communist elements also joined the Castro forces, and some may have infiltrated the 26th of July Movement's civilian underground as well.

Also of considerable importance was the underground apparatus of the Auténtico party which had been ousted from power on March 10, 1952. The Auténticos split into two groups, one led by Dr. Grau San Martín, which sought a "peaceful" resolution of the situation provoked by Batista, the other, loyal to exiled President Carlos Prío Socorrás, adopted an insurrectional attitude from the beginning. The latter group was led until 1955 by Prío's former Minister of Education, Aureliano Sánchez Arango. However, in that year Sánchez Arango had serious divergences with Prío, and established his own underground group, known as the Triple-A. It was particularly active in shipping in arms for use by the insurrectionists.

Another important underground was that of the Revolutionary Directorate. With its principal strength among the university students, the Directorate also had extensive contacts and some organization among the trade unionists. The Directorate was particularly active in carrying out individual acts of terror against members of the Batista clique. The most spectacular of these attempts was its unsuccessful attack on the presidential palace, in an effort to assassinate the dictator, on March 13, 1957.

For some time the Communists took an equivocal position toward Batista. Immediately after March 10, 1952, they hoped that the dictator, who lacked virtually all support in the labor movement, would turn toward them as he had done when he was in power before, so for several years the Communists maintained a position of benevolent neutrality toward him. It was not until the early months of 1958 that the official Communist party decided to throw in its lot with the rebels, and sent representatives to the Sierra Maestra to fight in Castro's army.

Meanwhile, large numbers of Communists joined Batista's party, the Partido de Acción Popular. Important Communists, including candidates for Congress in the 1952 election, suddenly turned up as members of the "workers' bloc" of Batista's party. Some of these individuals received important jobs in the administration, particularly in the Ministry of Labor.

The functions of the civilian underground were various. They carried out propaganda campaigns against the government. They raised millions of dollars from people in all ranks of life to purchase arms and supplies for the rebel armies. They built up skeleton groups in the trade unions which could call a general strike and seize control of the workers' organizations when the time was ripe. They gathered caches of arms for use during the final struggle against Batista.

The Batista Régime's Terror

After the launching of Castro's military insurrection, the Batista administration became increasingly violent in its persecution of the opposition. The terror was in the hands of the Military Intelligence Service (SIM) and elements of the civilian police.

The government's terror groups made sudden raids on houses of suspected underground leaders, rounding up anyone they found there. Union headquarters, business offices, the seats of such organizations as the Young Catholic Workers were raided and those found there were taken to police stations and army barracks.

The fate of many of those who were arrested was sealed as soon as they were picked up. Tens of thousands of people were submitted to vile tortures, and it is estimated that over twenty thousand civilians were killed in cold blood by the army and the police in waves of murders by the government forces. Events such as the unsuccessful general strike of April, 1958, resulted in scores of bodies being left in the streets in residential sections of Havana or being washed up on the shore each day. Many of these bodies were maimed beyond recognition.

The Culmination of the Anti-Batista Struggle

During the last months of 1958 the fight to oust the Batista dictatorship reached a climax. In April of that year, the underground forces had attempted to launch a general strike, but this failed, partly because of the arrest of some five hundred underground trade union leaders, but also because of poor organization and coordination among the anti-Batista groups and lack of preparedness on the part of the rank-and-file workers for a final move against the government.

After the collapse of the April general strike, Batista tried to make it appear that this failure had dealt a deathblow to the underground and insurrectional opposition. He went forward with his plans for the election of a successor in November, 1958, in spite of suggestions by many elements belonging to neither the government nor the opposition—including the hierarchy of the Catholic Church in Cuba—that some *modus vivendi* should be found for Batista's immediate retirement and the establishment of a transition government which could make peace with the armed rebels and pave the way for a democratic election to choose a new president.

The optimism of the Batista forces proved unjustified. The rebels began increasingly to venture out of the mountains from which they had hitherto operated, and by August, 1958, they had cut virtually all transportation between Santiago de Cuba, capital of the easternmost province, and the rest of the island. A month or so later, it was impossible for trucks, cars, and buses leaving Havana to go farther east than the central province of Las Villas.

In October a column from Castro's army, led by an Argentine

doctor, Ernesto Guevara, who was one of Castro's chief lieutenants, joined forces with the second-front rebels in Las Villas Province. During the following weeks, they captured most of the smaller towns of the province. Meanwhile, a third front was opened, largely by elements of the Auténtico party, in the westernmost province of Pinar del Rio.

During November and December, 1958, the provinces of Oriente and Las Villas came largely under the control of the rebels, while still another group of insurrectionists began operating in Camaguey, the province lying between Oriente and Las Villas. By the middle of December the rebel forces were laying siege to Santiago de Cuba and Santa Clara, capital of Las Villas Province.

The capture of Santa Clara during the last days of December, 1958, signaled the fall of Batista. There is no doubt that the sudden collapse of the dictatorship after this event surprised the rebels as much as it did many of Batista's supporters who were unable to join him in his flight into exile.

During the early morning hours of January 1, 1959, Fulgencio Batista, members of his family, and a group of his closest collaborators fled to the Dominican Republic, while others took off for the United States. Batista turned over power to a military junta, headed by General Cantillo, commander of the army garrison in Havana. Cantillo had been in secret contact with Castro's forces and had agreed to arrest Batista and other top officials of his régime when the dictatorship collapsed, but he went back on his agreement, and allowed the principal leaders of the dictatorship to get away.

Whatever ambitions Cantillo may have had of taking over effective control of the government from Batista were soon rendered abortive. As news of Batista's flight spread in Havana, armed members of the underground began to come out into the open. Their first acts were to seize such key installations as the power plants, radio and television stations, and police stations.

Meanwhile, the remnants of Batista's army in Camp Columbia, just outside of Havana, and the Cabana Fortress in the harbor of the city began to melt away, many soldiers deserting, others refusing to obey orders.

As a result of these events, Cantillo was left without any force with which to make his commands effective, and without any means of communicating his orders to the general populace. He was superseded within forty-eight hours by Colonel Barquin, named by Castro to take over immediate command of the Havana garrison. Meanwhile, the members of the underground, now converted into "militiamen," had effective control of the capital.

The Revolutionary Government

Although various groups had participated in the underground and insurrectional fight against Batista, Fidel Castro was recognized as the undisputed leader of the victorious revolutionary forces. His 26th of July Movement, with the approval of other revolutionary groups, had named former Judge Manuel Urrutia Lleo as provisional president of the Republic even before the fall of Batista. The day after Batista fled, Urrutia took the oath of office in Santiago de Cuba. Soon afterward he named his first cabinet, headed by Dr. Miró Cardona, former head of the Havana Bar Association, who had gone in exile during the Batista dictatorship. Other members of the cabinet were drawn from the ranks of the 26th of July Movement, and included several of Castro's guerrilla leaders.

The new government, which moved to Havana a few days after Batista's flight, announced its intention of first thoroughly purging the remnants of the deposed government, reorganizing the public administration, carrying out a series of reforms including a wide redistribution of land to the landless, and paving the way within a year and a half for democratic elections to get the country back on a constitutional basis.

Meanwhile, Fidel Castro leisurely proceeded from Santiago de Cuba toward the capital in a march reminiscent of an ancient Roman triumph. He was greeted by wildly cheering crowds everywhere he and his company stopped along the 1,500-mile route. Once in Havana, the victorious guerrilla leader set up his headquarters in Camp Columbia, the military encampment just outside Havana.

President Urrutia's first cabinet lasted just about six weeks. Then Prime Minister Miró Cardona resigned, saying that Fidel Castro, in whose hands power actually rested, should take the reins of office. He did so two days later, on February 16, 1959. Under his leadership, the government then began to put into effect its revolutionary program.

Although Castro's personal popularity with the masses of the Cuban people was extraordinary in the months following his victory, there was a certain amount of discontent against his rule among other revolutionary groups. This arose from several factors: Castro's unwillingness to recognize the part which revolutionary elements other than the 26th of July Movement had played in the struggle against Batista, and his insistence on the Movement's monopolizing the fruits of victory; his friendly relationship with the Communists during the first months he was in office; and his penchant toward being spellbound by his own eloquence.

The monopolistic tendencies of Castro and the 26th of July Movement were notable both in the government and the armed forces. Neither the Revolutionary Directorate, nor the Auténticos, nor the Ortodoxos were represented as such in the government. The armed forces of the 26th of July Movement became the national army, and the insurrectionists of all the other political groups were sent home soon after the overthrow of Batista. Few of them were incorporated into the new army.

These same monopolistic trends were notable in the labor movement. The 26th of July Movement seized control of virtually all unions, and industrial and provincial union federations as well as of the Confederación de Trabajadores de Cuba. The Castro government refused to allow those trade union leaders belonging to the Auténticos, Triple-A, and Ortodoxos who had fought against Batista but had been able to maintain office in their unions because of their solid rank-and-file support during the Batista period even to take part in union elections.

Union elections held in April and May, 1959, put most of the country's local unions firmly in the hands of members of the 26th of July Movement. Congresses of various national industrial union federations during the succeeding three months secured for Castro control over most of these groups.

The congress of the Confederación de Trabajadores de Cuba, which met in early November, 1959, marked a fundamental shift in the policy of the Castro government. At the meeting there was a struggle between anti-Communist elements of the 26th of July Movement, which had dominated the CTC and most of its unions since the 1st of January, and pro-Communist members of the Castro group. Fidel and his brother Raúl both intervened in the congress on behalf of the latter group, with the result that all but one of the leading anti-Communist figures were purged from the Executive Bureau of the CTC. Furthermore, a "purge committee" was established, for the purpose of removing the anti-Communist 26th of July leaders from control of the constituent unions of the Confederation.

The CTC congress coincided with other important events. One of these was the deposition and arrest of Major Hubert Matos, commander of the garrison in the province of Camaguey. Another was the disappearance of Major Camilo Cienfuegos, commander-in-chief of the revolutionary armed forces. Both of these men were known to be strongly opposed to any alliance between the Castro government and the Communists.

These events reflected a bitter conflict which had arisen within the Castro group. The first evidence of this struggle was the reorganization of the cabinet in June, 1959, which resulted in the dropping of Roberto Agramonte (who had been the Ortodoxos' candidate for president in 1952) as Minister of Foreign Relations. A second incident in this conflict was the threatened resignation of Castro as prime minister in July, 1959, which brought about the ouster and disgrace of Provisional President Urrutia.

Certainly, one of the issues in this internal quarrel in the Castro government was the attitude which should be taken toward the United States. The events of November coincided with the launching of a violent polemic by Castro and members of his government against the United States government. The U.S. was accused of having exploited Cuba for more than half a century, and was alleged to be preparing an invasion of the island. This campaign is still in progress as these words are being written.

Another subject of controversy within the 26th of July ranks was undoubtedly the question of a return to constitutional government. Right after his victory, Castro promised elections within eighteen months, but as time went on he became more and more reticent about setting a specific date for the reestablishment of a constitutional government. Finally, by the end of the year 1959, Castro was publicly accusing those who raised the question of elections of being "counterrevolutionary." He insisted that elections were "unnecessary," since he knew what the people wanted because of his constant contacts with them and the responses which he received from them at large public meetings from time to time.

Those who criticized the position of Castro on the election issue also pointed out that the freedom of the press and other means of communication was being increasingly curtailed. By the beginning of 1960 only unquestioning supporters of Castro were allowed access to radio and television, which had come completely under government control. At the same time, those newspapers which dared to criticize the prime minister were seized one by one, usually being taken over "in the name of the workers" employed in the enterprise. By September, 1960, none of the dozen and a half dailies in Havana dared voice any criticism of the régime.

At the same time the government took stringent measures to regiment the organized workers. By decrees issued during the first months of 1960, all collective bargaining was abolished, and all matters previously dealt with through collective negotiations were to be submitted to the Ministry of Labor for decision. At the same time, all employment of workers was transferred to the Ministry of Labor, and no worker could obtain a job except through its auspices.

The armed forces were used to bring recalcitrant workers into line. When a congress of the Construction Workers Federation in April, 1960, refused to obey the orders of the CTC purge committee to dismiss its leaders, soldiers were moved into the meeting hall and the congress was brought to a summary conclusion.

The nature of the agrarian reform which was undertaken by the government was undoubtedly another source of dispute within the 26th of July ranks. In the mountains Castro had promised to give the land to the landless peasants. The agrarian reform law which was passed early in June, 1959, provided both for granting freeholds to individual peasants and for the establishment of cooperative farms. In fact, virtually all land expropriated from large landholders was put into the hands of cooperatives, the managers of which were named by the Instituto Nacional de Reforma Agraria. The workers continued to receive wages as before, and the question of how the profits of these cooperatives would be distributed was left open for decision at a later date. Meanwhile the INRA was given virtually dictatorial control over what should be grown where, and a monopoly on the purchase and sale of most of the country's agricultural produce.

The agrarian reform was one aspect of a wide program of

social change launched by Castro. Other facets of this program were measures for the extension of education, the reorganization of the social security system, and the revision of the whole tax structure of the nation.

Although these measures enjoyed wide popular support and most of them were backed in principle even by revolutionary elements opposed to the 26th of July Movement, there was some concern among people both inside and outside the Castro group at the way in which they were carried out. There was also opposition to the "neutralist" and increasingly pro-Soviet tendencies of the Castro administration, and concern about attacks which Castro made on José Figueres Ferrer of Costa Rica, Puerto Rican Governor Luis Muñoz Marin, and others who had helped the anti-Batista movement considerably, but had criticized some aspects of the Castro government.

Summary and Conclusion

There is no doubt that the overthrow of Batista on January 1, 1959, was a remarkable victory for democracy in Latin America. It was one of the few cases in Latin American history in which a group of armed civilians had defeated a heavily equipped army in the field, and had overthrown a dictatorship based upon that army. The ousting of Batista was a victory for the people of Cuba.

However, the mere overthrow of Batista did not assure the establishment of democracy in Cuba. Castro was faced with a kind of temptation which became increasingly hard to resist. His tremendous popularity in the beginning and the almost slavish adoration of him by a large part of the population threatened to turn his head. His role as "spokesman for the people" and chief of the popular revolution seemed to bring him to believe that opposition to measures he proposes and to his own political ambitions are opposition to the revolution itself.

The downfall of Batista undoubtedly made possible the return of democracy to Cuba. The new leaders of the republic were presented with an opportunity to establish democracy on a firmer basis than ever before, by eliminating the corruption which had been the curse of all Cuban governments in the past. However, the future of democracy depends on the ability of Fidel Castro and the young men who led the revolution to remain loyal to the ideas which inspired them in the long struggle against the Batista dictatorship. As of September, 1960, they seem to be wandering further and further from these ideas.

The free elections promised by Castro have been deferred to an indefinite and unlikely future date. Freedom of dissent, while not entirely gone, has been greatly curtailed. No opposition parties or newspapers have survived. The democratic men around Castro have defected or have been imprisoned. Castro, who led the fight against Cuba's cruel tyranny, is now blowing out Cuba's brains, characterizing all dissent as counterrevolutionary, and allying his country with the biggest tyranny of all, the Soviet Union.

Has Castro passed the point of no return with respect to his tie-in with the Russian Communists, his violent anti-Americanism and his economic policies? For himself and his cohorts, the answer is probably affirmative, but for Cuba, it is clear that the long delayed and much needed social and economic revolution cannot and should not be undone in many respects. What Castro's critics must grasp is the difference between his anti-democratic and pro-Communist political policies and the vital economic and social reforms initiated by his régime to correct old and terrible evils.

Our belief is that Cuba has not passed the point of no return with respect to its journey toward Communism. Castro's original ideals made his leadership and his victory possible. These ideals of a government based on free elections and human rights still live in Cuba. They will be asserted again, soon, this time against the man who betrayed a great revolution.

CHAPTER NINE

SOME REMAINING
TYRANNIES
PART ONE:
THE TRUJILLO CASE

After January 1, 1959, when the government of General Fulgencio Batista Zaldívar fell in Cuba, there remained only three thoroughgoing dictatorships in Latin America. Only Generalissimo Rafael Leonidas Trujillo Molina of the Dominican Republic, General Alfredo Stroessner of Paraguay, and Dr. François Duvalier of Haiti were undisputed tyrants. A fourth ruler, Dr. Luis Somoza Debayle of Nicaragua, seemed to be torn between his desire to remain in power and his realization of the necessity to liquidate the dictatorship which he had inherited from his father, General Anastasio Somoza.

Of all the authoritarian rulers of the American Hemisphere during the present generation, the most violent, brutal, and absolute has been General Rafael Trujillo Molina. He has ruthlessly destroyed his opponents, and has converted his nation into a private estate, of which he is the undisputed "owner."

General Trujillo came from somewhat obscure origins, and received his first opportunity during the occupation of his country by the United States Marines during and after the First World War. At that time, the invaders sought to organize an army "to maintain law and order," but they had great difficulty in recruiting to it people of honesty and high caliber, since the new National Guard, as the army was called, was almost universally regarded as a puppet force for the occupying Marines.

Entering the new armed forces as a second lieutenant, Trujillo soon rose in the ranks, because of his undoubted intelligence, unflagging energy, and utter lack of scruples. Soon after the United States Marines left the country, he emerged as commander-in-chief of the army they left behind. This was the first step for the ambitious dictator-in-the-making.

Early in 1930 a revolutionary movement began against the government of President Horacio Vázquez. Although it could easily have put down this insurrection, the new army was surprisingly inactive. Its commander, General Trujillo, who shortly before had pledged his undying loyalty to the president, suddenly found that he was "neutral." Finally, in the face of the army's refusal to defend the constituted government, President Vázquez was forced to resign. A provisional régime was established and new elections were called.

Trujillo remained as commander of the National Guard and in effective control of the country. Never since has he given up this control. He was a nominee in the elections following Vázquez' resignation, and the forces which had been arrayed against one another in the recent revolt joined to name Dr. Federico Velazquez as a common candidate in the face of the threat of a Trujillo dictatorship. But Dr. Velazquez never had a chance. Thousands of his supporters were arrested, tortured, exiled, left dead in the streets or just "disappeared." By the time election day rolled around, there was little doubt that Rafael Trujillo would be "elected."

Since 1930 Trujillo has only once permitted the farce of an "opposition" candidate. All elections are unanimous. In recent years officials of his election board have not even bothered to differentiate between the total number of votes cast and the number voting for the candidates of the Dominican party, Trujillo's official political group. All elections since 1946 have been "unanimous."

Once in power, Trujillo organized a dictatorship which has not had its equal in recent times anywhere in Latin America. Many tools were used to make this tyranny effective. Fundamental was a secret police force which had eyes and ears everywhere. Over the years, Trujillo's "gestapo" has so intimidated the Dominican people that no one will trust even his best friend. Anyone who hears another engage in any kind of derogatory talk about the régime or its boss feels that he must report it, on the supposition that the one who has uttered these sentiments is an *agent provocateur* of the secret police and will report his "disloyalty" if he does not inform the authorities.

A few instances of the way in which the secret police of the Dominican Republic operates will make the matter clearer. A well known lawyer was standing outside of the city jail of the capital one day and saw a group of very young teen-agers, handcuffed to one another, being roughly pushed through the prison door by some police. He commented to the man standing beside him, whom he knew quite well, that this was "too bad." This man turned on him and accused the lawyer of disloyalty to the government and of discrediting the "generalissimo," to which the lawyer replied that he had not mentioned the generalissimo's name, that he did not feel that anyone as humble as he should do so in a public place.

This demeaning attitude was not enough, however, to save the lawyer from serious trouble. A few hours later, when he was eating supper, he was informed that the police were looking for him. He rushed to the home of the man to whom he had talked on the street, and found there the chief of the secret police, who immediately accused him of the most extreme statements against

Trujillo. Knowing that he might be shot on the spot for "defiance of authority" if he protested his innocence, the lawyer submitted to arrest without a word. Luckier than most of the victims of the Trujillo dictatorship, this man was allowed to go into exile a few days later.

In another case, an important official of the government was invited one evening to attend a fiesta in a local night club. Arriving late, he found there leading members of congress, high officers of the army, and other important figures in the government, all quite drunk. A group at the far end of the long table around which the celebration was taking place was engaged in a strident argument about some purely personal matter. Tired and not desiring to "paint the town," the official returned home, and thought no more about the party.

The next morning he was summoned to the generalissimo's office. Trujillo and the chief of secret police were present. Trujillo interrogated the man concerning the party of the previous evening, seeking to find out whether he or the régime had been the subject of the argument which the official had overheard. When Trujillo was finally convinced that the dispute had been purely personal, he picked up the phone, asked for the warden of the National Penitentiary and told him, "Let the men go." The official was sure that if the testimony which he had given had borne out Trujillo's suspicions concerning what had been discussed the previous night, the order would have been, "Take the men out and shoot them."

The secret police are ruthless toward those who arouse the enmity of the Benefactor. One of the authors knows of a formerly wealthy and influential family, now reduced to one person who was lucky enough to escape into exile after his father, mother, sister, and wife had all been killed by the secret police. In addition to the thousands of people who were killed in cold blood or simply disappeared during Trujillo's first campaign for the presidency, the process of eliminating all those who could possibly challenge the dictatorship or who got in the way of Trujillo's business interests has continued ever since. There is scarcely a family of any importance in the Dominican Republic which has not lost some member in this continuing purge.

The Trujillo terror machine has not confined its activities to the Dominican Republic. Many opponents of the government have been killed or have disappeared in neighboring nations. For example, Mauricio Báez, a refugee trade union leader, disappeared from Havana, Cuba, late in 1950; "Pippi" Hernández, a rich opponent of Trujillo, was shot in Havana in 1954; Andrés Requena, a Dominican-born United States citizen who edited an anti-Trujillo paper was murdered gangster-fashion in New York City in 1952. Several years earlier, another Dominican exile in New York, Sergio Bencosme, had suffered the same fate. Tancredo Martínez, a leader of the opposition Vanguardia Revolucionaria Dominicana, was luckier; he survived an attempted assassination in Mexico City in 1957.

The most famous case of disaster to a Trujillo opponent in a foreign country was that of Dr. Jesus de Galindez. He was a native of Spain, and representative of the Basque government-in-exile in the United States. A former resident of the Dominican Republic, he had written many articles against the Trujillo régime and had completed a book-length exposé on the subject when he suddenly vanished from the streets of New York City in March, 1956. Circumstantial evidence published in *Life* magazine and elsewhere has indicated that he was kidnaped and spirited away to the Dominican Republic in a plane piloted by an American, Gerald Murphy, after which no trace of him was ever found.

Gerald Murphy himself "disappeared" in the Dominican Republic, apparently because he knew too much and was threatening to disclose what he knew about the Galindez case. The Dominican government's explanation for his disappearance—that he had been murdered and his body thrown over a cliff by a

Dominican pilot, Octavio de la Maza, was not accepted by the United States Department of State, which is still insisting on a more adequate account of what actually happened to Murphy.

The secret police is not the only means of control which Trujillo possesses. He has a unique type of political organization, which is one of his key weapons. Only one political party is legal, the Dominican party, and the generalissimo is its chief. The national constitution, which Trujillo has had revised several times, provides that when a post in Congress becomes vacant, the head of the party to which the retiring official belonged is authorized to submit three names to congress, from which the house to which the man belonged must choose his successor. Since all members of Congress belong to the Dominican party, all nominations are made by Trujillo. It is his custom to submit the name of the man he really wants appointed at the head of his list.

This constitutional quirk is supplemented by Trujillo's custom of having all government officials submit to him an undated resignation before taking office. He is then in a position to "resign" any government officeholder at any time he pleases. Trujillo makes frequent and effective use of his "rights." It is not unusual for a Dominican officeholder to read about his "resignation" for the first time in the newspapers. And few people hold an office for very long. Perhaps the high point in Trujillo's game of musical chairs was reached when in one four-year term of Congress there was more than a 200 per cent turnover in members of congress, though there had been no elections during this period.

This merry-go-round of officeholders is not confined to civilian government officials. Trujillo uses the same tactics in the armed forces, not allowing any officer to become so well entrenched in any post that he can build up a following which might prove dangerous to the dictator. Thus Trujillo has not suffered from the problem which has plagued most other Latin-American dic-

tators—plots and counterplots organized by ambitious army officers who feel that they have as much ability and "right" to be
dictator as the man who is currently holding the job.

One of the most fascinating studies for those who know what
is going on in the Dominican Republic is to follow the fortunes
of various Trujillo henchmen through their "resignations" from
one job and appointments to others. One can tell from these
events whether an individual is going up in the scale in the Benefactor's favor or is on the way down to political oblivion and
perhaps even to physical disappearance.

In recent years, Trujillo has worked out a refinement in his
method of notifying officials that they are in trouble. Some years
ago he began writing "anonymous" letters to *El Caribe*, one of
his two newspapers in the capital city. These letters accuse some
high official of a bizarre collection of crimes against the state,
the generalissimo, and common morality and decency. Such a
letter is the cue for the "offending" official to write an abject
letter in reply, denying the accusations made against him, and
particularly emphasizing his undying loyalty and obedience to
the generalissimo.

Trujillo has demanded absolute obedience and subservience
from everyone of any importance in the Dominican Republic.
No meeting can be held dealing with any subject which does not
sing the praises of the dictator. More than one unfortunate person
has discovered that even though the subject under discussion has
no connection whatsoever with the generalissimo, he is in trouble
if he doesn't find some way of connecting Trujillo's name with
his subject.

If one does not pay proper obeisance to the generalissimo, one
is in constant danger of being labeled "indifferent." This is even
more dangerous than being a known nonconformist. One is likely
to lose one's job, find oneself guilty of various violations of health
regulations or of anything else the police choose to imagine, and
finally will be in jail. In tracking down those who are "indiffer-

ent" toward the régime, Trujillo assures that a desire to act against his government is nipped before it ever buds. Preventive terror is a hallmark of the Trujillo dictatorship and one of the principal explanations for its longevity.

One reason for the compulsory subservience of everyone to Trujillo is the dictator's extreme megalomania. The generalissimo early began to name the cities, towns, provinces, streets, plazas, and public buildings after himself or members of his family. As early as 1936 he had his puppet congress rechristen the city which Columbus named Santo Domingo. It became Ciudad Trujillo.

The capital city and all other urban areas of the country are spotted with monuments to Trujillo. On the famed Avenue of the United States Marines in Ciudad Trujillo there are two such within a few blocks of each other. One is an obelisk graven on four sides with praise of the dictator; the other is a more modest construction commemorating Trujillo's achievement of the "financial independence" of the country.

No organization can exist in the Dominican Republic without the permission and surveillance of the dictator. The trade union movement is typical. Although Trujillo has patronized the establishment of an extensive body of labor legislation, and has permitted the organization of the skeleton of the labor movement, these acts are largely for foreign consumption.

The lack of all trade union freedom has been commented upon by numerous observers. During 1958 a delegation of the International Confederation of Free Trade Unions, consisting of Daniel Benedict of the AFL-CIO and Raúl Valdivia of the Cuban Sugar Workers Federation, visited the Dominican Republic to study the labor situation. Its report commented on the utter lack of independence of the trade union movement and on the complete absence of collective bargaining contracts.

One of the authors had an experience which gave him a valuable insight into the way in which the Dominican trade union movement functions under Trujillo. During a visit to the country, he encountered an English-speaking Dominican trade unionist, who volunteered to take him to see his local union headquarters. The author accepted this invitation and spent an hour talking with members of the labor group. Later his English-speaking friend told the author that a group of men sitting in one corner of the union headquarters apparently playing cards had summoned him over to talk with them. They were, they told him, members of the secret police, and asked him who this stranger was who was asking too many questions. The Dominican worker would be in trouble if he didn't watch out, they added. The author's friend said that he did not know whether he would have a job, or even whether he would be in jail the next day.

Under such conditions, it is impossible for a real labor movement to function. The situation is particularly difficult in those industries directly owned by Trujillo, especially the sugar plantations. There not even the sham trade unions of the dictatorship are allowed and the workers are subject to the most ruthless exploitation for the benefit of the generalissimo. Labor legislation does not apply to Trujillo enterprises.

Rafael Trujillo has treated the Dominican Republic as his personal property. Virtually every source of income has been apportioned among the members of the Trujillo family. The dictator himself has taken over most of the island's principal industry, sugar, evicting numerous United States companies as well as hundreds of Dominican planters, small and large, in the process. Untold numbers of small farmers have been driven into dire poverty by the generalissimo's avarice.

All manufacturing enterprises have Trujillo or a member of his family as a partner. The two daily newspapers in the capital are his property while the radio and television industry belongs to a brother. One cannot go into business or stay in business in the Dominican Republic unless Trujillo is a partner. Even branches of powerful United States companies must pay regular

ribute to the dictator. One case of such tribute was brought out
y the U.S. Senate Finance Committee in July, 1957, when it was
iscovered that the Lock Joint Pipe Company of New Jersey
ad received a contract for a sewer and water construction job
1 the Dominican Republic only after adding $1,800,000 to its
riginal bid. Half of this addition went to Generalissimo Trujillo.
he witness commented that such payments were "an ordinary
nd necessary business expense" in the Dominican Republic.

Aside from the legitimate businesses into which the dictator
as cut himself as partner, the Trujillo clan has appropriated for
self many other less straightforward but equally lucrative
urces of income. Products imported into the Dominican Re-
ublic must pay three kinds of taxes—import duties, excise taxes,
nd a "special tax," which goes into the dictator's personal
easury. The vice business has been turned over to one of
afael Trujillo's brothers and gambling is a monopoly of another
ember of the Trujillo family.

Of course, no one but Trujillo knows how much all these
urces of income have brought in to him, but Germán Ornes,
ho has made one of the most authoritative studies of the Domin-
an dictatorship, has estimated that the private fortune of Gen-
alissimo Trujillo Molina amounts to at least half a billion dollars.

Trujillo and the Other Totalitarians

One of the sources of Trujillo's strength over the years has
een his ability to picture himself as the hemisphere's outstanding
pponent of communism. However, this is a mere pose. Trujillo
as over the thirty-year span of his rule been a friend not only
f the Communists but of numerous other kinds of totalitarians
d tyrants.

In the late 1930's, when fascism was riding high in Europe and
tending its influence in America as well, Trujillo was a friend
the European Fascists, but, always a shrewd judge of his own

best interest, he made the shift to the side of "democracy" early enough to avoid the wrath of the United States.

Soon after World War II, when many Latin American dictators were being overthrown and Trujillo had certain fears for his own safety, he entered into a short courtship with the Communists. His current term of office was expiring, and he felt the need to display some "democracy" and create an "opposition" to his reelection to the presidency.

A flirtation with the Communists served Trujillo's purpose at that time. So he sent an envoy to Cuba, where most of the exiled Dominican Communists were residing, and invited them to return home and legally organize their party. They took up his invitation, were repatriated, and began work in the general political field, as well as among the puppet trade unions. It is important to note that no other opposition group was allowed to renew legal activity in the Dominican Republic at this time, although Trujillo organized two "rival" political parties, each of which was allowed to "elect" a member of Congress.

While this was going on, Trujillo had his foreign office extend recognition to the Soviet Union. President Trujillo wrote a glowing letter to the foreign minister, praising the Soviet Union as a stalwart supporter of the "democratic cause" in the late war, commenting that communism was here to stay and had to be recognized, and noting that many Russian books, including some on communism, circulated in the Dominican Republic.

For a while, the Communists made considerable progress, particularly in the trade union movement and among the youth, who eagerly seized the opportunity to join a political group through which they could express at least some opposition to Trujillo. For several months the Communists suffered little hindrance from the dictator. They named candidates for the congressional election, which was to be held simultaneously with the choosing of a new president. Meanwhile, the puppet labor confederation of the Dominican Republic joined the Communist-controlled Confederación de Trabajadores de América Latina (CTAL).

But, before the scheduled election, Trujillo pounced upon the Communists. During a large public meeting of the Communists' Popular Socialist Party, a group of Trujillista rowdies attacked the crowd, there was a riot, and Trujillo used this incident as an excuse for suppressing the Communists. Most of the party's top leaders were able to escape through foreign embassies, but rank-and-file members throughout the country were arrested, were tortured, or disappeared.

This little episode with the Communists served Trujillo's interests in two ways. First, it provided him with an "opponent" during much of the election campaign and thus gave him an opportunity to claim that he had been "democratic." Second, since Trujillo allowed only the Communists to oppose him openly, he was able to claim that the sole enemies he had were the Communists. However, Trujillo's "anticommunism" was shown up in its true colors by this incident. The Dominican dictator is no more anti-Communist than he is devoted to any other ideological or philosophical idea. His ideology and his philosophy are summed up in one sentence: Keep Rafael Leonidas Trujillo in power.

Trujillo is still giving aid and comfort to the Communists, in spite of his pretenses to the contrary. This was made amply clear in April, 1960, when he again suggested to his puppet Congress that the Communist party be legalized in the Dominican Republic. It appeared likely that he was again preparing an elaborate pantomime with the Communists, similar to the one he had conducted a dozen years before.

Meanwhile, by accusing everyone who opposes him of being a "Communist," the Dominican dictator is adding to the prestige of the real Communists. He is doing his best to convince the people of the Dominican Republic that his principal enemies are the Communists, which is likely automatically to make them more popular among those in the Dominican Republic who are bitter against Trujillo than would otherwise be the case.

In recent years, Trujillo's friendship has been extended to

another kind of tyrant—the local Latin American brand. During the late 1950's several Latin American dictators were overthrown, and four of them—Perón of Argentina, Rojas Pinilla of Colombia, Pérez Jiménez of Venezuela, and Batista of Cuba—sought asylum in the Dominican Republic, which has been referred to by Chet Huntley of the National Broadcasting Company as "that refuge for past and present dictators."

Trujillo not only supports other Latin American dictators, but violently opposes the rulers of other nations in the area. This was indicated by two incidents which occurred during 1957 and 1958. Two gunmen picked up by the police of Costa Rica were accused of plotting to assassinate President José Figueres. During 1958 accusations that Trujillo had had a part in the assassination of President Carlos Castillo Armas were officially investigated by the Guatemalan Congress and largely upheld.

Trujillo and the United States

The Dominican dictator has long posed as "the best friend of the United States in Latin America," but it is clear that, like his "anticommunism," his friendship for the United States is a pose, or at best a matter of convenience rather than conviction. Trujillo has played ball with the United States only because it has suited his own purposes. And that it has served these purposes well, there is no doubt.

Trujillo has gotten aid in building up his already powerful armed forces. The United States has made available military planes and other equipment. In addition to this, the Trujillo government has won successive increases in the Dominican Republic's quota in the United States sugar market—a direct gain for the dictator himself, since he has most of the country's sugar plantations in his own hands.

Perhaps most important of all, from Trujillo's point of view, is the fact that his pose as "the great friend of the United States" has brought him fulsome praise from leading citizens and officials of the United States. Important members of the House of Representatives have gotten up in that august body to render panegyrics in praise of the Dominican dictator, echoing his assertion that he is a "democrat" and that only Communists oppose him. The same thing has occurred in the U.S. Senate. Late in 1958, two senators, Jenner of Indiana and Eastland of Mississippi, did Trujillo the honor of speaking before his puppet Congress and praising the dictator, while at the same time strongly attacking those in the United States who question his support of democracy and opposition to communism.

Praise of the Dominican dictator has come not only from members of the United States Congress. Most recent ambassadors of the United States in Ciudad Trujillo have talked more as if they were representatives of the Dominican Republic in Washington than the other way around.

Of course, all of the statements about the Dominican Republic by public figures in the United States have not been complimentary. Trujillo took due notice of this fact during the 1958 congressional election, when an official of his régime wrote letters to state party leaders, urging the defeat of four United States Congressmen, including one of the authors of this book. All four of these congressmen were reelected, in spite of Trujillo's best efforts—or perhaps because of them.

The shallowness of Trujillo's claims to be a great friend of the United States was amply demonstrated during the summer of 1958. The occasion was the failure of Trujillo's oldest son Rafael Jr. (generally known as Ramfis) to pass a course he had been following at the General Staff School of the U.S. Army, at Fort Leavenworth, Kansas. Almost simultaneously, Ramfis gained notoriety by expressing his love for actress Kim Novak while on a nation-wide television network, in spite of the fact that he had a wife and half a dozen children back in the Dominican Republic.

This combination of incidents served to raise the question of further economic and military aid to the Trujillo government during the discussion of the "foreign aid bill" which was then under way in the United States Congress. It was pointed out that Trujillo Jr. had spent in the United States, while he was supposedly studying at Fort Leavenworth, almost exactly the same amount which had been granted to the Dominican Republic in the previous year's foreign aid program. Some doubts were expressed concerning Trujillo's need for further aid.

All these circumstances aroused the unbridled ire of Rafael Trujillo Sr. As a result, the Dominican Congress, which was in recess, was suddenly called together to pass a resolution "authorizing" the president of the republic (Rafael's "little brother" Hector) to refuse to accept any more aid from the United States. Leading officials of the Dominican régime made statements asserting that if young Trujillo was not granted his diploma from Fort Leavenworth, the Dominican Republic would reconsider its policy of siding with the United States in the United Nations and elsewhere. This approach was simple international blackmail, but when the United States was not intimidated as Trujillo had apparently expected it would be, he announced that all that Congress meant to do was to "permit" the president to act according to the resolution, and not to "instruct" him to do so. He added that there seemed little likelihood that Congress' "permission" would be acted upon.

A new crisis in Trujillo's relations with the United States arose in the middle of 1960. An attempt to assassinate President Betancourt of Venezuela was traced directly to the Dominican government. As a result a special meeting of inter-American foreign ministers resolved on diplomatic and economic isolation of the Trujillo régime. The Eisenhower administration concurred in this move. However, it is notable that the U.S. Senate refused to authorize a cut in the Dominican sugar quota in conformity with the inter-American agreement.

The Opposition to Trujillo

No legal opposition to Trujillo is allowed within the frontiers of the Dominican Republic. Only once, at the end of and immediately after World War II, was even any pretense of opposition permitted. This was the period when Trujillo not only allowed but encouraged the Communists to establish legal organizations.

Although legal opposition is barred, this does not mean that Trujillo does not have any active opponents. In spite of all of the precautions of his secret police, there has always been an underground working against him. It was of particular influence during the late 1930's and in the immediate post-World War II period. It was perhaps weakest during the 1950's. However, after the fall of Batista, on January 1, 1959, the opposition grew stronger. Early in January, 1960, underground opponents of the régime were mounting a serious plot against the government, a move which Trujillo circumvented by arresting a reported 1,500 people. Many of those jailed were killed. However, Trujillo's success in this instance did not dishearten the opposition, which continued its efforts against the dictatorship.

This opposition is very active among Dominican exile groups abroad, who are organized into various parties and units. The oldest is the Partido Revolucionario Dominicano, headed by Juan Bosch, one of the country's outstanding literary figures. The PRD has local branches in New York City, Havana, Mexico City, Caracas, and other areas in which there are large numbers of resident Dominicans.

Another group, established in 1956, is the Vanguardia Revolucionaria Dominicana. The VRD, which is particularly strong among Dominican exiles in Puerto Rico and New York City, includes a number of distinguished professional men, and is particularly well informed on what is going on inside the Dominican Republic.

Other exile opposition groups include the Frente Unido

(United Front) and the Partido Populista (Populist Party). The Dominican Communists also maintain an active group among the exiles. After their falling-out with Trujillo, the Communists established their headquarters in Guatemala, but with the fall of Arbenz moved their seat of operations to Mexico City. They again shifted their headquarters, this time to Havana, after the fall of Batista.

With the exception of the Communists, all the Dominican exile groups are pledged to the establishment of a democratic government once Trujillo is overthrown. Most of them are members of what might best be called the Democratic Left. They are all carrying on a valiant and what sometimes seems to be a hopeless fight against Trujillo.

After the overthrow of Batista in Cuba on January 1, 1959, the activity of the exiled opposition to Trujillo was greatly increased. A series of new groups, called "patriotic juntas," were established among the exiles in Caracas, Havana, and New York City. In the two former cities these brought together Communists and the most conservative elements among the exiled opponents of Trujillo. The juntas received aid and encouragement from Castro adherents in Cuba, and they were the element responsible for the attempt made to invade the Dominican Republic in June, 1959. By early 1960 the Caracas Junta Patriotica Dominicana had split into rival Communist-dominated and non-Communist groups.

The June, 1959, invasion was headed by Captain Enrique Jiménez Moya, who had been an officer in the Castro Army. Several hundred young exiles participated in the attempt, which at first succeeded in temporarily capturing the town of Costanza, but was soon defeated by elements of Trujillo's army. The dictator's forces strafed and bombed a number of villages in which they claimed the rebels were hiding. Most of the invaders were killed, but a few escaped to the mountains in the western part of the country.

The failure of this rebellion did not reduce the nervousness of the Trujillo régime. It was followed by an unprecedented wave of terror against all elements of whom Trujillo had reason to be in the least suspicious. The most important victim of this terror was Ramón Marrero Aristy, Trujillo's Minister of Labor, who was reported by foreign newsmen to have some ideas about being a possible "compromise" successor to the dictator. He died in a mysterious "automobile accident" in a remote part of the country, a few days after a large group of foreign newspaper correspondents whom he had shown around the country had left the Dominican Republic. The "automobile accident" pattern was one which Trujillo had used frequently in the past to get rid of people who were annoying or dangerous to his dictatorship.

Meanwhile, Trujillo stepped up his attacks on neighboring republics. He lodged a complaint against Cuba and Venezuela in the Organization of American States, but withdrew it when he discovered that there was little sympathy there for his cause. He announced the formation of a "foreign legion" composed of ex-members of Franco's "Blue Division," and remnants of Fascist ex-storm troopers from several European countries. Such a group would seem to have little purpose but to attack one of Trujillo's neighbors. The high point of this Trujillo campaign was the attempt to assassinate Venezuelan President Betancourt in May, 1960.

During 1959 and 1960 Trujillo was certainly in more difficulty than he had faced at any previous time. The continuance of his dictatorship had come to be recognized by the democratic countries of the Caribbean as a standing menace to themselves, and Trujillo had become engaged in a war to the death with several of his neighbors. Although it did not seem likely that the technique used against Batista in Cuba was likely to prove useful against Trujillo in the Dominican Republic, cracks had begun to appear in the structure, and the days of the rule of the Benefactor seemed to be numbered.

CHAPTER TEN

SOME REMAINING
TYRANNIES
PART TWO:
PARAGUAY, HAITI, NICARAGUA

Although they are less absolute than the Trujillo tyranny, dictatorships still dominate the South American republic of Paraguay, West Indian Haiti, and Central America's Nicaragua. Each of these is worthy of some discussion.

The Origins of the Stroessner Government

Paraguay is a country which has seldom known political democracy. When independence was first established early in the nineteenth century, its first ruler was Dr. José Gaspar Rodríguez Francia, who enjoyed the title "Dictator for Life." Although a cultured man himself, he purposely cut his nation off from the outside world. He banned virtually all trade, he allowed what there was of an educational system to disintegrate, and he fiercely rejected friendship or even contact with other nations. At the same time, he used all the nation's resources to build as nearly a self-sufficient economy as was humanly possible, even establishing an iron and steel firm, which disappeared after his death and has never been revived. Needless to say, he allowed no opposition during his close to thirty years of rule.

Francia's policies were deliberate. He felt that his country, sandwiched between Argentina and Brazil, would not be able to maintain its independence if foreign influences were allowed to penetrate it. He ruled Paraguay with an iron hand, with no semblance of democracy. He created for himself the title of "El Supremo."

When he died, Dr. Francia was succeeded by a man of very different ideas, Carlos Antonio López. He opened up the frontiers, sent bright young Paraguayans abroad to study—including his own son, Francisco Solano López. He encouraged trade, and the country prospered during his administration. However, the rule of Carlos Antonio López, like its predecessor, was a dictatorship, though somewhat less ironbound than Francia's rule.

The third in Paraguay's list of tyrants was Francisco Solano López. Although he came into power in a beneficent atmosphere, Solano López dragged the country into perhaps the most horrible war which has ever occurred in Latin America. Under his leadership, Paraguay fought Argentina, Brazil, and Uruguay, and, before the conflict was over, a third of the population and virtually all adult Paraguayan males had been killed. The dictator himself was killed by a lance thrust.

During the next sixty years—1870-1930—Paraguay slowly recovered from the War of the Triple Alliance. During the last years of this period, the country seemed to be making steady progress toward economic prosperity and political democracy. However, this interlude was broken by another war, the Chaco conflict with Bolivia. Although Paraguay "won" this struggle, much of the progress which had occurred over nearly three generations was swept away, the economy was weakened, and the country suffered a new period of instability and dictatorship. Paraguay has not yet fully recovered from the Chaco War.

The end of the conflict brought revolution by the veterans who had fought in the bleak wilderness of the Chaco. They were led by Colonel Rafael Franco, one of the heroes of the war. In February, 1936, he established a "Socialist" administration, which encouraged the growth of a labor movement under strict government supervision, launched a program of distributing land to small farmers, and encouraged the development of the nation's economy. Franco was overthrown within a year, but his supporters formed the so-called Partido Febrerista (in honor of the month Colonel Franco seized power), and it became one of the country's three major parties.

Colonel Franco was followed by General Estigarribia, wartime commander of the army and also a hero of the war. He governed with the help of the Liberal party, and there was a considerable degree of civic freedom during his administration. He was succeeded by General Higinio Morínigo, who governed for eight years with the support of the majority of the army officer corps and with the Colorado party, traditionally the most conservative of the country's political organizations.

Morínigo ruled from 1940 until 1948. His was a dictatorship, although its intensity varied at different times. For a while late in 1946 and early 1947 Morínigo sought reconciliation of the country's various parties, and formed a coalition government with representatives of the Colorado, Liberal, and Febrerista parties. This attempt soon broke down, and in March, 1947, civil war broke out with the Liberals, Febreristas, and Communists, under Colonel Franco's leadership, attempting to overthrow Morínigo and the Colorados.

Morínigo won this civil war, and a few months later presided over an election in which there was only one candidate, Natalicio González, of the Colorado Party. González was ousted less than a year later by a rival faction of the Colorados and the army garrison of the capital, Asunción. His successor was Dr. Federico Chávez, whose dictatorship in turn was ousted by still other

Colorados and the same army garrison. The leader of this revolt was General Alfredo Stroessner, who was "elected" president in July, 1954, in a poll in which he was the only nominee.

The Nature of the Stroessner Administration

At the time of Stroessner's "election," there was some hope among opposition parties that he might modify the army-Colorado dictatorship. However, nothing in this direction was done until late 1957. At that time, negotiations were opened between the government and the Liberals. The upshot was that the Liberal party was able to hold a convention in Asunción for the first time in many years in July, 1952. However, by October of the same year most of the Liberal leaders were back in exile.

Throughout his first term, President Stroessner kept thousands of Liberals, Febreristas, and other opponents of his government in exile, the secret police remained all-encompassing, and there was little freedom of speech, press, or assembly. Oppositionists accused his police of brutally torturing political prisoners. There were only two limited exceptions to this situation—in the labor movement and in the university.

Although it suffered severe restrictions, the labor movement was for several years allowed by Stroessner to function more freely than most other social and political groups. The trade unions had been badly disorganized during Morínigo's administration, but had been allowed to reorganize and form the Confederación Paraguaya de Trabajadores during the administration of Dr. Federico Chávez.

The CPT was closely associated with the Colorado party, or one faction of it. All the top leaders of the organization and its affiliates had to belong to this party, though Liberals and Febreristas participated in the unions and even held minor posts. The Communists were not allowed to have any degree of participation in the leadership of the labor movement.

However, early in 1959 the government crushed the Confederación Paraguaya de Trabajadores, as a result of several strikes to
which the government was opposed. The top officials of the CPT
were jailed and removed from their official positions. Appointed
government stooges were put in to run the unions. The limited
effectiveness of the Paraguayan labor movement was completely
destroyed, and the actions of the government were strongly con-
demned by the International Confederation of Free Trade Unions
and its regional organization, the ORIT (Inter-American Regional Organization of Workers).

The student body of the University of Asunción has been one
of the principal strongholds of opposition sentiment throughout
Stroessner's period of administration. Liberals, Febreristas, and
Communists all have had supporters among the students, and they
not infrequently have made their existence known. However,
insofar as the faculty of the university has been concerned, the
government has been careful to see that only loyal Colorados
are employed.

In 1958 General Stroessner had himself "reelected" in a plebiscite, in which he ran unopposed. Paraguay remained a one-party
state, with the ultimate power in the hands of the army, and
particularly the Asunción garrison.

On the positive side, the Stroessner régime has continued the
economic and social policies of its predecessors. The program of
distributing land to small farmers, which had been started by
Colonel Franco and continued by all of his successors, has been
furthered by Stroessner, and he has encouraged a modest program
of industrialization and general diversification of the economy.

The Future of the Paraguayan Dictatorship

The Paraguayan opposition took heart from the fall of the
dictatorships of Argentina, Venezuela, and particularly of Cuba.
However, although the general atmosphere in Latin America is

favorable toward the abolition of the few remaining dictatorships, the downfall of Stroessner in the near future is by no means certain. There are important factors both favoring and working against his disappearance from the scene.

For a while there was some indication that General Stroessner himself might try to pave the way toward a gradual evolution of a more democratic administration. Late in 1958 he announced his intention of allowing municipal elections, with the participation of the Liberal and Febrerista parties as well as the Colorados, but the failure of the attempted *rapprochement* with the Liberals in 1958 soon raised doubts concerning these declared intentions of the dictator.

Stroessner's attitude may have been influenced by a split which developed in the ranks of the Colorado party in 1958 and 1959. Important elements of the dominant party were increasingly annoyed by the army's role of "ruler behind the scenes." Many Colorados were also disgusted with the Stroessner régime's crushing of the labor movement. This growing opposition within the Colorado party culminated in June, 1959, in a vote of censure of the government by Congress, which Stroessner countered by dissolving the legislative branch and arresting many of its members.

Growing opposition to the leadership within the Catholic Church is a factor militating against the continuation of the dictatorship. In February, 1958, Father Ramón Talavera denounced from his pulpit the plebiscite which the president called to secure his reelection. A month later Archbishop Juan José Anibal Mena Porta of Asunción urged the faithful in a pastoral letter to call on President Stroessner to start a policy of national reconciliation and civic peace. On several subsequent occasions, the Church censured actions of the government.

There are strong factors militating against an end to the dictatorship. Such an event can come in only one of three ways: by action of Stroessner himself, by a *coup d'état* of the army, or by invasion by exiles. The first alternative is problematical at best. The second is possible, but past history indicates that there is not a great deal of likelihood that an army *coup d'état* will result in the establishment of a democratic government. It is more likely to mean the supplanting of the dictatorship of Stroessner by that of some other ambitious military man.

The possibility of invasion by some of the thousands of Paraguayan exiles is not to be completely discounted. However, its likelihood was greatly reduced in 1958 by a *rapprochement* between the Argentine government and Stroessner. The provisional governments which succeeded Perón had not been friendly toward Stroessner because of his friendship for Perón and his having given refuge to the deposed Argentine dictator. Relations had been coldly formal at best, and Stroessner himself had tended to court Brazil in order to counterbalance the hostility from Buenos Aires.

However, the inauguration of President Arturo Frondizi in Argentina in May, 1958, changed all this. For reasons best known to himself, Frondizi decided to improve relations between his country and Stroessner's. In October, 1958, he made a state visit to Paraguay, decorated Stroessner, and generally made it clear that he wanted no quarrel with the neighboring dictator. Since any invasion of Paraguay by exiles must come from Argentina, this *rapprochement* between Buenos Aires and Asunción reduces very greatly the possibility of success in the near future of this method of overthrowing the Stroessner government.

The Background of the Duvalier Dictatorship in Haiti

Haiti is particularly handicapped in the struggle for democracy. It has the highest degree of illiteracy of any country in the hemisphere. Its poverty is the deepest and most nearly universal of any American nation. Its history has been largely an alternation between chaos and dictatorship. The existence of the

Trujillo tyranny across its eastern frontier is a constant threat to any attempt to establish democracy in Haiti.

This by no means signifies that there is no aspiration for a democratic government or that the country is "not prepared" for it. Although very poor, the great majority of the Haitian population is proud and self-reliant, a situation brought about in part at least by the fact that most Haitians own at least a little piece of land, and one period in recent history, the years 1946-1950, has indicated that democracy is feasible in Haiti.

United States Marines occupied Haiti from 1915 until 1934 and after their withdrawal the country lapsed into the dictatorships which had characterized it before World War I. However, in January, 1946, President Elie Lescot was overthrown by a military coup, which paved the way for elections, which were won by Dumarsais Estimé, a former schoolteacher.

Estimé's administration was, by and large, a democratic one. Political parties were established for the first time—including a Christian Social party, an indigenous party comparable to the Aprista or national revolutionary parties in other Latin American countries, the Mouvement Ouvrier Paysan; and a Communist Party, which functioned under the name of Parti Socialiste Populaire. There was a wide degree of freedom of the press, speech, and assembly. The government encouraged the growth of a labor movement for the first time. In the economic and social field, it pushed energetically a program of economic development and enacted the country's first labor legislation, including a minimum wage law and the beginnings of a social security system.

The Estimé government set afoot for the first time in Haiti several modern currents which none of its successors was able to overlook completely. Aside from being an experiment in political democracy and giving rise to institutions such as political parties and trade unions which might help to lay a firm basis for democracy, it also gave expression for the first time to the desires so widespread in other underdeveloped countries for economic development and social justice.

In spite of his democratic record during most of his administration, President Estimé made the mistake of attempting to change the constitution to permit his own reelection. This provoked another army *coup d'état*, led by General Paul Magloire. After a short period of "provisional" government, General Magloire had himself elected president without opposition.

General Magloire's régime was a dictatorship. The political parties were suppressed and there was little freedom of the press. There was only one opposition member of Congress during much of this period, Daniel Fignolé, head of the former Mouvement Ouvrier Paysan. General Magloire allowed a limited amount of freedom for the labor movement, and continued the social policies of the Estimé administration, laying particular stress on a workers' housing program, which was largely in the blueprint stage under Estimé.

Magloire made the same mistake as his predecessor, and in December, 1956, sought to make possible his continuation in office after the expiration of his term, but he was overthrown as the result of a "strike" by the merchants of Port-au-Prince, which provoked an army coup against him. During the next seven months there was a period of rapidly changing government.

In May and early June, 1957, it appeared as if stability as well as democracy might return to Haiti's government, when Daniel Fignolé became president. He enjoyed widespread support among the masses of Port-au-Prince and other cities as well as among the peasants. He announced his intention of calling elections as soon as possible, and during his few weeks in office got the government machinery—which had virtually ceased to function—into operation once again, including the process of tax collection.

After Fignolé had been in office three weeks he was deposed

because the army leaders were not in sympathy with the popular trend of the government, which threatened to take from them the power to make and unmake governments at will. The army dissidents then went ahead with "elections" in which only one candidate, Dr. François Duvalier, was allowed to campaign. Fignolé and Louis Dejoie, who were also candidates, were in exile. A fourth nominee, Clément Jumelle, was in hiding with a price on his head.

The Nature of the Duvalier Régime

Duvalier took office in October, 1957. Since that time he has ruled with an iron hand. Showing little gratitude to the army officers who had put him in power, he drove most of the top military men into exile. Real power was in the hands of the *cagoulards* or "hooded ones," a group of toughs organized by Duvalier to terrorize his opponents, who descended on suspected or known enemies of the government in the middle of the night and beat them up or even killed them.

No semblance of party political activity has been allowed by Duvalier. There is not even any pretense of freedom of the press. The labor movement has been all but wiped out and its leaders have been killed, jailed, or exiled.

Duvalier has developed close relations with his neighboring tyrant in the Dominican Republic. Late in 1958 he signed an agreement with Trujillo, allowing him to move Dominican troops into the country if the "national sovereignty" of Haiti were endangered, as unpopular a measure as any Haitian chief executive could ever conceive of making.

At the same time, Duvalier successfully sought the help of the United States. Not only did he receive economic aid, but he requested and received the dispatch of a mission of United States Marines to "train" the Haitian army, which had been virtually destroyed by Duvalier's terrorism. Apparently neither Duvalier nor the United States government officials involved were aware of the inevitable effect which the presence of a Marine mission would have in recalling the ill-fated occupation of Haiti by the same foreign military force a generation ago.

Meanwhile, opposition to Duvalier continues. No amount of repression has been sufficient to destroy completely the underground organizations of the opponents of the dictatorship. The most extreme methods were used. Thus, a brother of former presidential candidate Clément Jumelle was shot down in the streets of Port-au-Prince by the *cagoulards*. Jumelle himself died because he was unable to receive adequate medical care after taking refuge in a foreign embassy. In April, 1959, Duvalier threatened to break off diplomatic relations with Venezuela, because two other political opponents had taken refuge in the Venezuelan Embassy in Port-au-Prince.

The opposition to the Duvalier administration is divided into three main groups, those which had been organized to support the presidential candidacies of ex-President Daniel Fignolé, Clément Jumelle, and ex-Senator Louis Dejoie. Each of these groups has support among the people of Haiti, though they are of different political orientations and backgrounds.

Jumelle was Minister of Labor and Minister of Finance under President Magloire. Although he served a dictatorship, he was largely responsible for carrying out the social policies of that régime, and built up a considerable amount of support among the urban masses, particularly among the trade unionists. He was the unofficial nominee of Magloire in elections scheduled for early 1957, but was betrayed by the dictator's attempt to perpetuate himself in office. Jumelle died early in 1959, and his brother Gaston took over the leadership of his group.

Louis Dejoie was a senator under Magloire, and represents the more conservative interests of the capital and other cities. His basic strength is among the merchants of Port-au-Prince, whom he led several times in political protest stoppages between December, 1956, and October, 1957. He is a very conservative man, denounces the political and social policies of Estimé as having been demagogic, and talks a great deal about the need for "re-establishing order" in Haiti.

Daniel Fignolé was Minister of Education for a short while under Estimé, but broke with him for personal reasons. Subsequently, he organized a trade union movement which had particular influence among the country's sugar plantation and refinery workers. He also organized a political party, the Mouvement Ouvrier Paysan, which functioned throughout the Estimé administration. Fignolé's trade union movement and political party were both suppressed by Magloire, but the dictator was forced to recognize Fignolé's election as deputy for Port-au-Prince in the national Congress. Throughout the Magloire régime, Fignolé harassed the dictatorship from his seat in the chamber.

With the overthrow of Magloire, Fignolé again began organizing his followers in support of his candidacy for the presidency. He toured the country from one end to the other, and won wide backing from the small peasants, who are the backbone of the nation. In all likelihood, had honest and free elections been held after the fall of Magloire, Fignolé would have been chosen president by a sizable majority.

Various attempts have been made to form a united front of the opposition to Duvalier. Late in 1958 such unity seemed to be achieved, with the formation of a United Democratic Front among the exiles in New York. However, after the overthrow of Batista in Cuba, Louis Dejoie went to that island and carried on propaganda and organizational activities among the many thousands of Haitians resident in the eastern end of Cuba. At the same time, he repudiated the united front agreement, apparently feeling that he would have the support of the new government of Prime Minister Fidel Castro in his attempt to oust Duvalier, and therefore needed no alliance with any other Haitian opposition group.

Prospects for Haitian Democracy

The struggle for democracy is particularly handicapped in Haiti. The country is one of the most primitive in the Western Hemisphere. Poverty, overpopulation, illiteracy, and lack of any great reservoirs of natural resources make it exceedingly difficult to achieve the minimum level of economic well-being which might be thought of as essential to a successful functioning of democracy. The almost complete lack of democratic experience on the national level would also seem to militate against the future existence of an administration based on free elections, and guaranteeing the individual the liberties of speech, association, and press. Most of all, perhaps, the proximity of Trujillo's "private hacienda" next door militates against the triumph of democracy.

The innate pride of the Haitian common folk, dating back to the time their slave ancestors achieved freedom from their French masters, is a source of possible strength for democracy. So is the small landholding system, which reduces to the minimum the individual's dependence on a powerful neighbor for his livelihood. Finally, the contacts of those members of the élite among whom politics is largely conducted, with the outside world—the United States and neighboring Latin American countries—are a factor favoring the ultimate triumph of a democratic government in Haiti. This small republic no longer lives in relative seclusion as it once did, and the events in neighboring countries around the Caribbean will undoubtedly have an impact upon it.

In contrasting ways, the recent experiences of the country under Estimé and Duvalier should also strengthen the ultimate chances for democracy in Haiti. The administration of Estimé is still looked back to, ten years later, as one of the best periods in the country's history, even by many who were not friends of Estimé when he was president. The people of the towns and cities enjoyed a freedom which they have not had since, and something concrete was done to advance the economic and social situation of the great masses of the rural population. This was a period of hope which is remembered with nostalgia.

On the other hand, the Duvalier régime has outstripped all its recent predecessors in the intensity of its oppression and terror. Although it seems likely to persist for some time to come, it may well go far to convince all elements of the opposition of the need for a leadership which is respectful of the rights of the individual and which derives its claim to power from the fact of election by a majority of the people.

The Government of Anastasio Somoza in Nicaragua

The dictatorship which has ruled Nicaragua for a quarter of a century was the heir of the occupation of the country by the United States Marines during the 1920's. This occupation was made famous by the long-drawn-out guerrilla warfare between the Marines and General Augusto B. Sandino, who refused to recognize the right of the American soldiers to be in his country.

In order to aid in the fight against Sandino and leave a national armed force behind once the United States occupation was over, the Marines organized the National Guard of Nicaragua. With the withdrawal of the United States forces, the National Guard became the national army of Nicaragua, and General Anastasio Somoza became its commander-in-chief.

Somoza, who belonged to the Liberal party, which controlled the Nicaraguan government, used his position as army commander to acquire control over the government itself. However, before this could be complete, he had to get rid of General Sandino, who was by now a national hero. Sandino was invited to come into the capital, Managua, to negotiate an end to the long guerrilla conflict. Sandino agreed, an accord was reached between him and the government, but he was assassinated before he could return to his own armed forces. At that time, and for as long as he lived, Somoza was accused of arranging the assassination of Sandino, a charge which he never effectively refuted.

General Somoza became provisional president in December, 1936, upon the resignation of the incumbent. He remained in control of the government from then until his assassination in September, 1956.

Anastasio Somoza's government was a dictatorship, but in many ways it was a milder one than many of those in Latin America in recent years. During some periods Somoza allowed a certain degree of freedom of speech and even of the press, and if the opposition didn't try too hard to depose Somoza, they were allowed to live comfortably in their homes. More frequently than not, Somoza was able to strike a bargain with the leaders of the principal opposition party, the Conservatives.

However, more principled and energetic opponents of Somoza were brutally treated by the dictator. These consisted largely of groups of young people unaffiliated with either of the two traditional parties. Most of these younger opponents were in jail or in exile during most of the dictatorship of Anastasio Somoza, where they have remained since his death. They now constitute the bulk of those seeking to end the tyranny of the Somoza dynasty.

The Somoza dictatorship was not as notorious as some others in the area for the use of terrorism and torture against its opponents. Somoza was reported in the late 1940's as expressing disgust at the heavy-handed methods of Trujillo and as having suggested that the Dominican dictator was mentally unbalanced.

Somoza knew how to bend with the prevailing political winds. During World War II, when Nicaragua, like all of the other American countries save Argentina, was an "ally" of the United States, and there was a great deal of thought and discussion concerning "postwar reconstruction" in all the countries involved in the war, he adapted himself to the situation. He had a labor code enacted, permitted the development of a labor movement, and allowed a wider degree of political freedom than had existed previously.

During this period, Somoza made an arrangement of convenience with the Communists. After a visit to Nicaragua by Vicente Lombardo Toledano, head of the Communist's hemispheric trade union apparatus, he allowed them to establish legally the Partido Socialista de Nicaragua. He also allowed them to get the upper hand in the newly established labor movement. In the election of 1947, he sought to reach a deal with the Partido Socialista on a joint ticket for members of Congress. When this failed, however, he quickly suppressed the Communists.

For several years after Somoza's break with the Communists, he did not permit the reestablishment of a labor movement, in spite of his labor code, but in 1949 local unions were allowed to reorganize once again. Several central labor organizations were also organized, all of which—except a small group under Communist control—were loyal to Somoza, though they represented different ideological currents. For a short while the Peronistas were in the ascendancy in the Nicaraguan labor movement, but even before the fall of the Argentine dictator, Peronista influence had seriously declined.

Only once was Somoza in serious difficulty. This was immediately after the election of 1947. Deciding that the circumstances called for him to give up the presidency temporarily, he threw his support behind Leonardo Arguello, an old man who had aspired to the office for a generation, but had always been passed by when it came time to choose a Liberal nominee. Somoza apparently felt that because of Arguello's age and his gratitude to Somoza for having finally made his dream come true, Arguello would be a pliable tool of the dictator. To be doubly sure, Somoza assumed command of the army when he retired from the presidency.

Arguello turned out to be a sad disappointment for Somoza. He quickly made it clear that he intended to be president in fact as well as in name. He promptly ended certain special privileges which Somoza the ex-president had extended to Somoza the businessman. He "exiled" Somoza's son, Anastasio Jr., an army officer, to a remote garrison town. There were even rumors that Arguello intended to relieve Anastasio Sr. of his command.

Before Arguello could move directly against him, Somoza unseated the president, whose term of office lasted only twenty-six days. He was succeeded by Victor Soto y Román, a relative and faithful servant of Somoza. In spite of the fact that the other republics of the hemisphere refused for a year to recognize the Soto y Román government, Somoza won out, and reestablished the security of his régime. With the next presidential election, he again assumed the post of chief executive, which he held until his death.

Somoza treated his country as if it were his private ranch. One could not enter into business in the republic without making him a silent partner. He was the country's largest rancher, the most important investor in industrial establishments, the principal grower of sugar. He is once supposed to have defended his use of political power for personal enrichment by remarking that because of his interest in business he had built up the nation's economy, and that unlike some other Latin American rulers, he had invested all the money he made in his own country.

There is no doubt that Nicaragua experienced a considerable degree of economic development under Somoza. The government pushed roads into areas which had previously been virtually isolated from the outside world, thus putting them in contact with markets for their goods for the first time. In these efforts he received considerable help from international lending institutions. The Somoza régime also encouraged the diversification of agriculture, and particularly the development of sugar and cotton growing. Industrialization was not overlooked, and by the time of Somoza's death there was a variety of factories in Managua and other cities, including textile plants, sugar refineries, breweries, shoe factories, and other plants.

Somoza frequently quarreled with his neighbors. Border feuds with Honduras were reopened from time to time. After the

Costa Rican revolution of 1948 which deposed Rafael Calderón Guardia and Teodoro Picado, friends and business associates of Somoza, his relations were particularly bad with the southern republic. Twice he helped the Calderón and Picado forces to invade their homeland from Nicaraguan soil.

The Second Generation of the Somoza Dynasty

Anastasio Somoza Sr. was assassinated in September, 1956, while at a reception in his honor in the city of Leon. His position as president was taken over by his son Luis, who had been president of Congress until his father's death. Anastasio Jr. continued in the post of commander of the armed forces to which his father had named him some time before.

Although the death of the old dictator was followed by the arrest of large numbers of possible opponents of the régime, many of whom were tortured, Luis Somoza gave some indications in the beginning of his administration that he intended to bring the dictatorship to an end. In 1958 he announced that he felt that no relative of the president should be a candidate for the presidency in the next election, scheduled for 1962. A law to this effect was passed late in 1959. Meanwhile, the government allowed a rather wide degree of freedom of press and speech. Visitors to Nicaragua found no difficulty in hearing strong criticism of the régime in private conversations, and the press and even the radio began to criticize the government more frequently and more vigorously than in the past.

The overthrow of the Venezuelan and Cuban dictatorships increased the pressure on Somoza. Soon after the victory of the Castro forces in Cuba and the inauguration of Rómulo Betancourt as president of Venezuela early in 1959, President Luis Somoza made some interesting comments on the general situation in the Caribbean. He noted that in that part of the world there were two kinds of governments, one which he qualified as "liberal" such as those of Castro and Betancourt, and the other which he called "reactionary" such as the Trujillo administration. He added that he considered his government to be in the former rather than in the latter category. His words were greeted with a certain degree of sarcastic response in other Caribbean countries.

Some people inside Nicaragua and abroad are convinced of Luis Somoza's desire to put an end to the dictatorship which has ruled his country for nearly twenty-five years. However, many have doubted that Anastasio Somoza Jr., a professional soldier and reportedly a man of much more authoritarian tendencies than his brother, would be willing to permit free elections which might end the rule of the Somoza dynasty.

These doubts are shared by many hundreds of Nicaraguans who still remain in exile, principally in Costa Rica, Cuba, and Venezuela. These exiles took heart early in 1959 from the overthrow of Batista's dictatorship in Cuba, and the assumption of power in Venezuela of Rómulo Betancourt, whose sympathy for the people of American countries still suffering under dictators is well known.

The opposition to the Somozas was undoubtedly growing rapidly inside the country during the first months of 1959. The labor movement, which had been benevolently neutral toward the government of Anastasio Sr., became increasingly hostile to his successors. Large elements of the business community also turned against the government, and brought pressure on the Somozas to resign.

The opponents of the government, like those of Trujillo's, are divided broadly into two groups, those of pro-Communist sympathies, and those of a democratic orientation. The former group has its principal center of influence among the exiles in Cuba; the latter is strongest in Nicaragua and among the exiles in Costa Rica and Venezuela. Both groups are actively working to overthrow the Somoza dynasty, convinced of the futility of trying to seek a change from within the régime.

At the end of May and during the first days of June, 1959, a serious attempt was made by the group based in Costa Rica to oust Somoza by force. Exiles invaded Nicaragua, and their action was seconded by a general strike (with employer support) within the country. However, Luis Somoza declared martial law, and the invaders, who had landed in wild and virtually empty country with which they were not familiar, were unable to make any military progress. The general strike collapsed, and the revolutionary attempt was abortive. Meanwhile, other exile elements coming from Cuba, who had landed in Honduras near the Nicaraguan frontier, were prevented by the Honduran army from joining the military action.

The Future of the Somoza Government

The Nicaraguan régime remains in June, 1960, one of the few dictatorships still in power in Latin America. The unstable situation which has existed since the death of Anastasio Somoza Sr. is not likely to last much longer. There seem to be two likely alternatives in the near future. The first is that the Somoza dynasty will be displaced by some more democratic government, either of its own volition or as the result of a violent change. The second is that, through the initiative of Anastasio Somoza Jr., or by agreement of the two brothers, the régime will become more authoritarian and the relaxation of reins which occurred after their father's death will be ended. Whether this will save the Somoza dictatorship or not is another question.

CHAPTER ELEVEN

THE UNITED STATES
AND THE STRUGGLE FOR
DEMOCRACY IN
LATIN AMERICA

The United States, as the richest, most powerful nation in the Western Hemisphere, and as a champion of the principles of democracy, has a great responsibility in the struggle for democracy in Latin America. Although it has no moral or legal right to intervene directly in the internal affairs of its neighbors, its influence in the New World is so great that it cannot help but have some effect on this struggle. It behooves this country to see to it that its influence is used on the side of democracy rather than to help dictatorships. Unfortunately, in the recent past, the reverse has frequently been the case.

Background of Present-Day Inter-American Relations

In order to get a proper perspective on recent United States attitudes toward the struggle for democracy in Latin America one must go back at least as far as the time of Presidents William McKinley and Theodore Roosevelt. It was during that period that the United States adopted the policy of the Big Stick, and asserted its Manifest Destiny in the hemisphere.

We made war on Spain, ostensibly to free Cuba, and ended up by establishing Cuba as a virtual protectorate and annexing Puerto Rico as a colony. We helped to engineer a revolution in the Colombian province of Panama, and within three days recognized the independence of that area as a separate republic. Very soon afterward we signed a treaty with the new republic, which gave us rights to build a canal through its center under conditions to which the Colombian government had refused to agree.

We began the policy of ousting governments of several Latin American republics because they would not or could not pay their debts, using as an excuse the claim that if we did not intervene some European country would. We began a policy of giving unquestioning support to any United-States-owned enterprise which got itself in trouble in any of the Latin American republics, regardless of the cause of its trouble or the justness of its case.

Of course, all of these things are "just history" now, but they are worthy of mention because they are still vividly remembered by the people and politicians of Latin America, and are the background against which a still lingering distrust of our motives and actions persists.

The Good Neighbor Policy

Our policy toward Latin America began to change with the administration of President Herbert Hoover. He had traveled widely in Latin America, and during his service as Secretary of Commerce had taken considerable interest in trying to improve relations with the Latin American republics. As President, he began the policy of withdrawing United States troops from the various republics where we had them stationed, and under his leadership the first steps were taken toward a declaration by the United States that it recognized the juridical equality of the Latin American countries.

It was during the administration of Franklin D. Roosevelt that the most fundamental alteration in our policies toward the other American republics occurred. It was during this period, too, that relations between this country and Latin America were the best that they have been during the present century, and perhaps in all our history.

President Roosevelt had promised to establish a new attitude toward Latin America, an attitude of "The Good Neighbor." After a few false steps very early in his administration, he, Secretary of State Cordell Hull, and Under Secretary Sumner Welles set about to make this new policy effective.

During the twelve years of the Roosevelt administration the Good Neighbor Policy consisted principally of four points: full recognition by this country of the juridical equality of the Latin American countries with the United States; renunciation on our part of the right to intervene in the internal affairs of the other American countries; alignment of these countries in a joint attempt with us to secure military, economic, and political protection against attempts of the Axis powers to penetrate the American Hemisphere; and the beginning of a policy of economic and technical assistance to the Latin American nations in meeting, first, the problems of the world depression and World War II, and second, the problems of economic development.

President Roosevelt and Secretary Hull over and over again reiterated their belief that the sovereignty of the Latin American countries was no less absolute than our own. They repudiated the Manifest Destiny concept that the United States had a special right to dominate the hemisphere.

A corollary to this idea was the renunciation by Roosevelt and Hull of the right of the United States to intervene in the internal affairs of the Latin American nations. This policy of nonintervention had several facets. In the first place, we unilaterally re-nounced the Platt Amendment, which Theodore Roosevelt had forced the Cubans to incorporate in their constitution, giving us the right to unseat the Cuban government under certain condi-tions, and the right to determine when these conditions existed. Second, nonintervention involved the withdrawal of United States troops from Haiti and Nicaragua, where they were still stationed when Franklin Roosevelt took office.

Third, and perhaps most important of all, the new concept of nonintervention meant that the United States was no longer willing to use armed force or even to use heavy political pressure to back up United States firms, regardless of why or how these firms had gotten themselves into trouble in Latin America. It meant a recognition of the right of the Latin American nations to order their own economies, with the United States reserving only the same right that it would have in any nation of the world, to protest if United States firms or individuals were being treated in a discriminatory way and were not getting the same rights extended to anyone else under similar circumstances.

This aspect of the Good Neighbor Policy was put to two hard tests in the cases of the expropriation of the Standard Oil Company holdings in Bolivia in 1936 and of several United States and British oil companies in Mexico in 1938. Much pressure was brought to bear on President Roosevelt to intervene or at least to "punish" Bolivia and Mexico through diplomatic and economic pressure. He resisted this pressure, and specifically recognized the right of those countries to expropriate, asking only that the United States firms involved be treated fairly. These incidents went far to convince the people of Latin America that Roosevelt meant what he said about nonintervention.

Another basic aspect of the Good Neighbor Policy was the development of procedures for joint consultation among all the American republics concerning developments both within the hemisphere and abroad. Within the hemisphere, the policy was

adopted of sounding out the other American governments when-
ever a violent change occurred in the régime of any one of them,
before recognizing the new government. With regard to events
outside the hemisphere, the United States sought to get the other
American republics to present a solid front against the attempts
by Nazis, Fascists, and Japanese to establish political, economic,
and military beachheads in the New World. Joint defense ar-
rangements were made with the Latin American countries even
before the United States entered the Second World War, and
there was the closest cooperation between this country and most
of the Latin American nations during that conflict—the only
major exception being Argentina.

Finally, the Good Neighbor Policy saw the beginning of a
program of economic and technical aid to the Latin American
countries. One step in this direction was the policy toward Cuba,
and the enactment of the Sugar Act in the middle 1930's, assuring
the Cubans—and other suppliers of sugar to this market—of a
reasonable percentage of the market and what, for then, were
decent prices for their product. Subsequently, during World
War II, the United States entered into an agreement with the
coffee-producing countries of the hemisphere to try to limit the
shock which the war would have on their basic industry.

The establishment of the Export-Import Bank in the middle
1930's represented a new departure, too, in the economic relations
of the United States and Latin America. It set about very early
in its career to make loans to some of the Latin American countries for the purposes of economic development. During the Second World War it made very important loans to Chile, Mexico
and Brazil, for instance, to establish basic iron and steel industries
and made a variety of other loans to help in the growth and
diversification of the Latin American nations' economies. The
Eximbank has continued this policy since the war, though no
on the scale which perhaps might be wished for.

An extensive technical assistance program also got under way a program which served as a model after 1949 for the Point Four program throughout the world. Through the Office of the Co-ordinator of Inter-American Affairs, technicians, training, materials, and other help were provided for improving health, bettering educational systems, improving labor relations, and aiding industrialization of the Latin American nations. This was continued in the Institute of Inter-American Affairs, now part of the State Department.

Lack of Adequate Policy Since World War II

Unfortunately, the good start made in improving our relations with Latin America under Franklin D. Roosevelt has not been continued since his death. For the most part, Latin America has tended to be ignored. The United States has been understandably concerned with events in Europe, in Asia, and most recently in Africa. It has, therefore, tended to take Latin America for granted, and when it has paid attention to the other American republics, the United States has seemed generally to have had the attitude that it was principally concerned with avoiding trouble in the region. The Latin American boat should not be rocked, regardless of who seemed to be in command of it.

Only when a crisis has occurred in some particular country has the top leadership of the United States for a short moment paid some serious attention to our policies in relation to the Latin American nations. Such crises were the violently vituperative campaign of Perón against this country in 1952-1953, the Communist situation in Guatemala in 1954, the troubles of Vice President Nixon in 1958, and problems with Cuban Prime Minister Castro in 1959-1960. Each of these aroused furtive interest and some soul-searching, but the excitement soon died down. Typical is the fact that the suggestions of Vice President Nixon, provoked by his experiences in his tour of South America in May, 1958, seemed to have had little effect on United States government policy, at least insofar as political problems of the hemisphere were concerned.

As a result of this attitude of taking the area for granted, there have not been any very well defined guidelines to United States relations with Latin America since 1945. The region has seldom, if ever, been mentioned in speeches of the President and the Secretary of State, and their interest in the areas has seemed largely to consist of enunciating platitudes or trying to shove something down the throats of the Latin American delegates to international conferences. (Some change in this pattern was shown by Secretary of State Herter during the Special Inter-American Conferences in Santiago, Chile, in August, 1959, and in San José, Costa Rica in 1960.)

Even the Assistant Secretaries of State for Latin American Affairs have not been able, for the most part, to enunciate a coherent and consistent policy with regard to our relations with the other American republics. Of course, the responsibility for such a policy is not theirs but that of the President, Secretary of State, and other top officials of the government. One Assistant Secretary who tried to establish some basic principles of Inter-American relations, John Moors Cabot, was removed after only a year in office in 1953-1954.

The upshot of this has been a series of bewildering zigzags in our policy.

Influence of Pressure Groups on United States Policy

The explanation for the inconsistencies in our policies toward Latin America seems to the authors to be the fact that, lacking any over-all policy to follow in the area, the State Department and other officials charged with conducting our affairs in the other American countries have been subject to an infinite variety of pressures. They have tended to give wherever the pressure was hardest at any particular moment. They have often been unable to reject pressure, even when they felt that the things they were being asked to do were wrong, because they have not been able to base such rejection on a stated and clear policy on the part of the United States government. If there had been such a policy, it would have been possible for them to reject pressures which ran counter to it, making clear that what was being demanded was inconsistent with the United States' over-all objectives in the Latin American area. Lacking such objectives, the best of the State Department officials were often hard pressed to do things which they knew quite well were wrong and could only damage our relations with the other American republics.

These pressures have been of a very diverse sort. Perhaps the single most powerful pressure group since World War II, insofar as Latin American policy has been concerned, has been the United States armed forces. As is logical in view of their profession, the leaders of our armed forces have tended to look at Latin America only from a military point of view. They have wanted good relations with the military men of Latin America, no matter who they were or what they represented in political terms. They have wanted agreements which would seem to bind the defense of the respective Latin American countries a little more closely to that of this country. They have wanted to train people from the Latin American armies in U.S. techniques, in the use of U.S. arms, and to indoctrinate them with the military notions which are in vogue in this country.

This is all understandable, but it should not have been the overriding consideration in our relations with the Latin American nations. The basic problem in Latin America during these years has certainly not been military, but rather political and psychological. It has been one of winning the friendship of the peoples of these countries and of their democratic political leaders. If we turn the people of Latin America against us, as they *are* being turned against us, because of our close association with the military dictators who, unfortunately, have all too often been in the

saddle in Latin American countries since 1945, whatever agreements we make with the Latin American military will prove to
be but scraps of paper.

Though the authors do not pretend to be military experts, they
cannot help but have grave doubts concerning the efficacy of
any agreements which may be made with most of the Latin
American armies, navies, and air forces—particularly armies.
Fundamentally, the security of the Latin American countries
from attack from outside the hemisphere depends upon the
strength of the United States armed forces. Very few of the
Latin American armies could resist an invasion by a first-rate or
even a second-rate power for more than a few hours at very most.

These armies have little to do in defending their countries
against their immediate neighbors, since the Inter-American system now in existence has shown itself rather efficient in snuffing
out internecine warfare in the area, and it will be efficient so
long as the United States is of preponderant strength in the
hemisphere. Furthermore, it is certainly not to our advantage, or
to that of the Latin Americans to arm these countries to fight one
another.

The chief potential danger to security in the hemisphere, then,
comes from possible difficulties within the Latin American countries themselves. To be more specific, it comes from the possibility that pro-Communist or neutral-against-the United States
régimes will come to power in one or another country. This
possibility is greatly intensified by the existence of military dictatorships. Recent experience in Cuba, Peru, Colombia, Venezuela,
and elsewhere has demonstrated that the Communists were much
stronger after these dictatorships than they had been before them.

The Latin American armies, which are of little use in actually
defending their nations, are highly effective in tyrannizing over
their own civilians. To the degree that we help them to do so
by arming them, bemedaling them, and otherwise supporting
them, we are weakening the defense of the hemisphere, not
strengthening it.

One can cite many instances in which the United States armed forces have exerted pressure in determining policy in Latin America so as to favor the dictators. Certainly, the granting of the Order of Merit to dictator Manuel Odría of Peru and dictator Pérez Jiménez of Venezuela in 1954 was a case in which the pressure of our armed forces won out over the best judgment of the State Department. Our continuing to have a military mission in Cuba, training Batista's soldiers to fight Fidel Castro's rebels throughout the Cuban Civil War, is another. Still a third was the granting of the Order of Merit to General Tabernillas, commander of Batista's air force and the man in charge of smuggling for the Batista régime. A fourth case of military pressure was the move of the United States Navy to send three admirals to the Dominican Republic at a time when that dictatorship was being menaced by invading revolutionaries, in the summer of 1959. Early in 1960 the navy further backed Trujillo by choosing Ciudad Trujillo as the port at which to give shore leave to 4,000 U.S. Marines on maneuvers in the Caribbean. Much of the zigging and zagging in our relations with Perón were also undoubtedly attributable to the influence of our armed forces.

American business elements active in Latin America, or desirous of becoming active there, also have sometimes brought pressure to bear in a way that has not helped the relations of this country with the Latin American peoples, and which has favored the dictators. Pressure of United States businessmen was exerted in behalf of the Perón régime upon several occasions. Businessmen with interests in the Dominican Republic, have been stanch supporters of the Trujillo dictatorship. The oil companies, which received extensive new concessions during the Pérez Jiménez rule—concessions which they had not been able to extract from other administrations for more than a decade—undoubtedly helped to create a friendly attitude toward that Venezuelan dictatorship. United States businessmen in Cuba were among the most fervent and vocal supporters of the Batista dictatorship.

Infrequently, the United States labor movement has been able to bring enough pressure to bear to influence the United States government's action in such a way as to favor the democratic elements in Latin America. For example, this was the case at the time of the invasion of Costa Rica by troops from Nicaragua in January, 1955. Several months before, President José Figueres of Costa Rica had notified representatives of the United States labor movement that such an invasion would occur. The labor leaders involved alerted the State Department to the situation, and were promised that if the invasion occurred without any concurrent uprising within Costa Rica itself, the United States would do all in its power to get the Organization of American States to intervene rapidly to stop the attack by Nicaragua. The State Department was as good as its word. When the invasion took place, the United States used all its influence to get the Organization of American States to back Costa Rica and to order Nicaragua to withdraw its troops. Somoza took the hint and the invasion collapsed.

Sometimes disinterested groups of United States citizens concerned with the problem of democracy in the hemisphere can bring pressure to bear on United States authorities. Most outstanding among these organizations is the Inter-American Association for Democracy and Freedom, headed by Miss Frances Grant. Through publicity, contacts with State Department and other government officials, and maintaining close relations with the democratic governments of Latin America, it has helped to counter the forces favoring the dictatorships.

It can even be maintained that officials of the State Department have themselves acted as a pressure group upon occasion. This, it seems to the authors, has been true in the case of United States treatment of Bolivia since 1952. That republic is perhaps fortunate that its capital, La Paz, has an altitude of 14,000 feet, and, therefore, the Bolivian ambassadorship is not one avidly sought by defeated candidates for public office or large campaign contributors. The upshot has been that since 1952 the United States has had a succession of very good career ambassadors in La Paz. They have been men who have been well aware of the significance of the revolutionary changes which have been going on in Bolivia since 1952 and have had sympathy for the efforts of this little country to catch up with history. They have, therefore, supported consistently a policy of extending moral, political, and economic support to the government which has been presiding over this change. The United States policy toward Bolivia is one of the bright spots in the Latin American picture during recent years.

Unfortunately, the policy of having no policy in Latin America, and leaving the decisions on each issue up to the various pressures which happen to be applied on the State Department at any given time have more often than not resulted in a questionable pattern of behavior by the United States in inter-American affairs since 1945. It has generally meant the support of dictatorial régimes against democratic elements, it has meant a fitful and inconsistent attitude with regard to economic aid to the area, and above all, it has meant taking Latin America for granted.

United States Support of Dictators

United States support of dictators in Latin America has often been explained away by State Department officials, many of whom the authors are sure have been exceedingly unhappy about the matter themselves, as merely a policy of "nonintervention." They have argued that the United States cannot intervene, even on behalf of democracy, in the internal affairs of the Latin American countries.

This is a weak excuse for supporting dictators. The people who offer it must be well aware that the United States is of such preponderant size and importance in this hemisphere that anything it does or does not do has a strong influence on the Latin

American nations. We "intervene" in a way whether we wish to do so or not. Furthermore, we have not generally tended to be merely neutral toward dictatorial régimes; we have *positively* aided the dictators.

The case of Perón is characteristic. After the failure of Ambassador Spruille Braden's hostile policy toward Perón in 1945, the United States did a complete turnabout. From then until Perón's fall, we followed an almost continuous policy of friendship toward the dictator. We gave him two loans, one in 1951 to clear commercial accounts, another in 1955 to build a steel plant. Between the time one revolutionary attempt against Perón had failed in June, 1955, and the second succeeded three months later, a top official of the United States government, on being received by Perón, made a speech comparing him with Lincoln to the disadvantage of Lincoln.

The situation with regard to other countries was in some cases even more flagrant, though perhaps less widely known. For instance, the United States was consistently friendly toward General Manuel Odría, who in 1948 overthrew one of the few democratically elected presidents that Peru has had in the twentieth century. This support was shown not only when we extended economic help to his government, but when we decorated him with the Order of Merit, and accompanied the decoration with a citation praising him for his "fight against the Communists and other subversive elements." This phrase, "other subversive elements," was widely interpreted in Peru to mean the Aprista party, the majority political organization in the country, until recently the only organized democratic party in Peru, and a party with a thirty-year history of fighting the Communists on their own ground, among the workers, the peasants, and the intellectuals.

We followed a similar policy toward an even more brutal dictator, General Marcos Pérez Jiménez of Venezuela. At least one of our ambassadors saw fit to become an intimate friend of

Pedro Estrada, the head of the National Security Police, a man who could perhaps have taught lessons to Beria and Himmler on how to run a political police. This same Estrada was received with full honors when he visited Washington. We also decorated Pérez Jiménez with the Order of Merit, congratulating him on his policies "before and after becoming president"—policies which included overthrowing a democratically elected régime, suppressing the trade union movement, maintaining one of the world's most brutal concentration camps in the steaming Orinoco River Valley, canceling the counting of election ballots when it became clear that his supporters had been defeated and then proclaiming himself, "in the name of the armed forces," president of Venezuela.

For a period of twenty years we have been exceedingly friendly toward the Somoza dynasty in Nicaragua. As late as June, 1959, the United States ambassador in Nicaragua chose to become virtually a mouthpiece for the Nicaraguan government in denouncing an attempt to overthrow the Somoza dictatorship. The founder of the Somoza dynasty, Anastasio Sr., was welcomed to Washington with open arms, and his régime was the beneficiary of a considerable amount of economic help—principally designed to build roads to the plantations which he had accumulated in various parts of the country.

One of our most recent adventures in support of Latin American dictators has been that in Haiti. The administration of President François Duvalier in that republic has been one of the most tyrannical which Haiti has had in this century. It is maintained in power largely by the operations of a civilian terrorist group known as "the hooded ones," who beat up, imprison, and kill opponents of the dictator in the dead of night.

We have seen fit to give Duvalier extensive economic aid, and, much worse, to send a military mission consisting of United States Marines to Haiti to rebuild the army of that country, the army destroyed by Duvalier because he feared its ability to oust him. The idea of sending a Marine mission to a country which for twenty years was occupied by the United States Marines passes all understanding. The mission was requested by Duvalier, but one would have thought that those in charge of our relations with Latin America would have been aware of the implications which this mission would have not only for the Haitians, but for all the rest of Latin America. Rightly or wrongly, this is certainly interpreted as a renewal, at least in part, of the policy abandoned when the Marines were withdrawn from various Latin American countries a quarter of a century ago.

The intervention on behalf of a dictator which has caused most embarrassment in recent years was our support of Batista. We continued to send him arms to use against Fidel Castro's rebels for fifteen months after the rebellion began. We continued to have a military mission in Cuba, training Batista's army right down to the day the dictator fled. Although United States officials announced that this mission was training the Cuban army to fight foreign foes, the fact was that the foes they were fighting were Cubans who were trying to oust an exceedingly brutal dictatorship. We did this in spite of clauses in the military agreements with Cuba which made it possible for either party to cancel the agreement if the other became engaged in a civil war. If we were really concerned with democracy in the Hemisphere, the United States government would have cancelled both arms aid and the training mission as soon as it became clear that civil strife had broken out in Cuba.

Finally, the most disgraceful and inexplicable case of all is that of the Trujillo régime in the Dominican Republic. We have suffered more indignities at the hands of Trujillo than from any other ruler outside the Iron and Bamboo Curtains. He has pursued his political victims even in this country; he has had people kidnaped from New York and spirited to the Dominican Republic and he has openly intervened in a United States election, seeking to persuade the heads of their parties in their respective states

to repudiate four candidates for Congress in the 1958 election.
He has had his Congress grandiloquently say that it would not
accept any more aid from the United States if it didn't give his
good-for-nothing playboy son a certificate for a course which
he had seldom attended. He forced most of the United States
firms doing business in the Dominican Republic to sell their
holdings to him.

This is the world's worst dictatorship. Not in any of the Iron
or Bamboo Curtain countries is the terror exercised by the government over the populace as great as it is in the Dominican
Republic. Trujillo has killed, sent into exile, or bought off virtually every opposition leader in the country. He has such an
efficient spy system that people cannot trust their own families
or closest friends. He has made a fine art of the process of
humiliating even his own closest associates. He keeps them in
constant fear of ouster from office, imprisonment, and even
death.

Yet, in spite of this situation in the Dominican Republic, and
in spite of the insults and vilifications which Trujillo and his government have hurled at the United States government and at
some of its highest officials personally, the United States remained
strangely silent until the summer of 1960. To the authors' knowledge it directed two letters of protest to the Dominican Republic
concerning the death of the American aviator Gerald Murphy in
the Dominican Republic in December, 1956, but that is all that
the public knows about the United States' attitude toward the
case. No protest was made against the meddling of Trujillo in the
United States election of 1958. There is little indication that the
United States regards the Dominican Republic as being any less
worthy of our friendship and cooperation than, let us say, the traditional democracy of Uruguay.

If ever there was a case in which the United States could make
clear its dislike for a Latin American dictator without being

accused of "intervention," it was the case of the Dominican Republic. We could do this on the basis of the things which Trujillo and his régime have done to the United States and to citizens and residents of this country. Yet, for some reason or another, this has never been done. Instead, our ambassador in the Dominican Republic signed his name to a flowery statement of praise of the Trujillo régime which appeared early in 1959 as a paid advertisement of the Dominican Government in the New York *Herald Tribune*.

In June, 1959, the United States ambassador had his picture taken shaking hands with an aviator whom the Dominican government claimed it had used as a double agent to entice exiles back to their death in the Dominican Republic. An official explanation was given by the State Department that the ambassador did not know who the man was with whom he shook hands—although the Dominican press and radio had announced beforehand that the aviator was to be presented to the diplomatic corps.

Our occasional backing of democratic administrations, as in the case of Costa Rica and Bolivia in recent years, has not been enough to offset our general attitude of friendship and support for the dictators in Latin America. It is not surprising that many Latin Americans look upon our general protestations of belief in democracy as hypocritical. They are inclined to think that we are perfectly happy with dictators unless, as in the case of Guatemala, they are an immediate menace to this country. Latin Americans can hardly be blamed for thus interpreting our attitude, and for their increasing tendency toward "neutralism."

Insufficient Economic Aid

For democracy to have a firm basis in the Latin American countries, it is necessary for these nations' economies to grow sufficiently so that the people of Latin America will have a decent standard of living. All the countries of the area are now engaged in attempts to diversify their economies, to industrialize, and to provide better living conditions. They realize that the United States, if it wishes to do so, can help them greatly in making economic development occur more rapidly and in a less painful manner than might otherwise be the case.

During the Second World War the United States made extensive promises—or gave the Latin Americans the impression that it was making extensive promises—that after the war this country would go all out to help them achieve their objective of rapid economic development. By and large, they feel that they have been deceived, and there is considerable justification for this feeling. In this field, as in political matters, United States policy since 1945 has been inconsistent and sometimes contradictory.

It is true that the Export-Import Bank has continued to make loans to the Latin American countries. Most of these were for the purpose of specific development projects, but many of them were to clear commercial debts to United States exporters. It is also true that the Point Four organization under its various changes of name has continued and expanded the program which was started under the Coordinator of Inter-American Affairs during World War II. It is also a fact that United States funds have gone to the Latin American countries through the International Bank for Reconstruction and Development and through the International Monetary Fund. Finally, it is true that there has been some private investment in Latin America since the war, particularly in the petroleum industry.

Unfortunately, there has been little semblance of an over-all plan or program in our economic aid. All too frequently the United States has held off until a country has gotten into particularly tight circumstances, has been faced with an excruciating foreign-exchange crisis, has piled up large commercial debts in this country, and then the United States has made available loans to clear up these commercial debts to United States exporters.

Often, to get even this, the governments of some of the Latin American countries have had to agree to economic measures within their own countries which were politically exceedingly dangerous and might well result in the overthrow of the existing administration. Such a case is that of Argentina under President Arturo Frondizi.

Our inconsistency and lack of planning in the field of economic aid to Latin America was demonstrated in the early 1950's in the case of Brazil. The United States and Brazil established a Joint Economic Commission, which, after making a survey of the Brazilian economy, drew up a general plan for development. It also suggested the establishment of a Brazilian Development Bank, and a program of long-range United States economic aid, to be extended through the bank, to help Brazil deal with some of the bottlenecks which are seriously hampering the growth of the economy of the largest of the Latin American countries.

Soon afterward, the United States agreed to allocate $500,000,-000 of the funds of the Eximbank for this purpose. This money would take the form of loans for a number of separate development projects, to be decided on by the Joint Brazilian American Commission and to be administered through the Development Bank. All this was decided upon in the last part of the Truman administration, and was an exceedingly hopeful turn in the economic relations of this country with the Latin American nations. Some $180,000,000 was actually allocated under this scheme.

However, soon after the Eisenhower administration took office, Brazil was faced with one of its periodic foreign exchange crises, and owed approximately $300,000,000 in commercial debts to United States exporters, on current account. So the United States government announced that it was extending a loan of $300,000,-000 through the Eximbank, and that it considered, therefore, that its commitments to the Brazilian development program had been entirely met.

This announcement caused an enraged outburst from the Brazilian press, including the newspapers most friendly to the United States. The United States was accused of going back on a solemnly made promise, since the commercial debts cleared by the $300,000,000 credit had nothing directly to do with the agreed-upon development program, and should have been handled as an entirely separate matter.

For ten years or more the United States held out against two suggestions which were constantly and urgently made by Latin American spokesmen: the establishment of an Inter-American Development Bank, and the setting up of procedures for stabilizing the prices of the principal Latin American export products. These suggestions might have been two essential cornerstones of a well-thought-out economic policy for the United States in the Latin American area, but they were rejected over and over again by this country in innumerable Inter-American conferences.

Finally, in the summer of 1958, both of these measures were accepted by the United States, shortly after Vice President Nixon had suggested that more attention be paid to economic aid to the Latin American nations. However, as one United States government official told one of the authors, it was all "too little and too late." It was announced in a routine press release of the State Department, whereas it might have been put forward by the President or Secretary of State as the commencement of a new attitude by the United States toward Latin America. It was announced almost as if we were ashamed of the fact that we were finally giving in on something which the Latin Americans had urged for so long. There was little indication that this meant a real change of heart on the part of this country.

In the summer of 1960 the U.S. Government proposed a somewhat expanded program of economic aid, offering to provide half a billion dollars for help in developing the social services and some basic economic projects of the Latin American nations. This program was discussed at a special meeting of inter-American finance minister in Bogotá in August, 1960. Perhaps it indicates a growing realization by the United States of the pressing economic needs of the other American republics.

Thus, in its economic programs, too, the United States has tended to be indecisive and really to lack an over-all policy in its dealings with Latin America. The long-range economic plans of the United States are no clearer than the long-range political plans, as far as Latin America is concerned.

The Present Crisis in Inter-American Affairs

The United States' lack of a well defined policy in the Latin American field has led to a major crisis in Inter-American relations. If the situation continues to deteriorate for many more years as it has in the last few, it will not be long before any Latin American political leader who dares publicly to express friendship for the United States will be generally regarded by his fellow citizens much as the members of the Pétain régime in France were regarded by most patriotic Frenchmen during World War II.

The situation has become acute because of the fall of half a dozen dictators since September, 1955. The régimes of Perón in Argentina, Odría in Peru, Rojas Pinilla in Colombia, Lozano in Honduras, Pérez Jiménez in Venezuela, and Batista in Cuba have been overthrown in one way or another. The remaining dictatorships of the Somozas in Nicaragua, Stroessner in Paraguay, Duvalier in Haiti, and Trujillo in the Dominican Republic find themselves in increasingly difficult circumstances.

One result of this overthrow of the dictators has been the release of the feeling of resentment against the United States and its political and economic policies in Latin America, which could be only partially expressed so long as the dictators remained in power. In most cases, the United States was fortunate that the principal leaders of the opposition to the dictatorships were convinced democrats and men who were pro-United States in spite of our policies, because they understood the broader issues involved. It is ironical that many of these people, who were frequently denounced in our press during the period of the dictatorships as "Communists"—such as the Aprista leaders in Peru and Rómulo Betancourt, now president of Venezuela—are today, in fact, the best friends that the United States has in Latin America.

These leaders of the democratic Left in Latin America are increasingly faced with a new kind of opposition, which we may call the Jacobin Left. This new group is exceedingly impatient for social change. Its members are fanatically nationalist and are unbending in their hostility toward the United States. As a result of these attitudes, these new Jacobins have no patience with any attempt at a *rapprochement* with the United States, or even with liberal elements in this country. Neither do they wish to "waste time" by following democratic procedures or constitutional forms.

This group has appeared within the ranks of some of the parties of the democratic Left in various Latin American countries, though it remains a minority group within those parties. However, its existence gives added importance to the developments in Cuba after the fall of Batista. Fidel Castro is the most prominent single representative of the Jacobin Left. His appearance on the Latin American political scene has given hemispheric leadership to this tendency throughout Latin America.

The situation which developed in Cuba after the overthrow of Batista created a much more difficult problem for the future of inter-American relations. When the remaining dictatorships are overthrown—and particularly with the downfall of the Somozas and Trujillo—the situation brought about by the Cuban events will in all likelihood get still worse.

A good deal of friction has developed between the Castro régime and the democratic Left political parties such as the Peruvian Apristas, the Acción Democrática party of President

Betancourt in Venezuela, and the Liberación Nacional party of ex-President Figueres of Costa Rica, which are nationalist and for social reforms, but are democratic in philosophy and are with the United States in the Cold War. This combination of circumstances might well present the United States for the first time with an important group of Latin American states which were frankly unwilling to take sides in the world-wide struggle.

The situation in Nicaragua and the Dominican Republic is particularly disturbing. The dictators of both those countries have boasted loud and long of the friendship of the United States for them. The United States has done little to prove this boast untrue. At the same time, Trujillo and the Somozas have equated all their enemies with the Communists. This is likely to have exceedingly bad results when the present régimes are overthrown in those countries.

In the Dominican Republic, it has been thirty years since there has been any real political controversy. The people of the country are likely to be completely "innocent" of the problems of the world in general, and the problems which are likely to face their own country once the dictator is gone. There is not the political sophistication which exists in Cuba which is the best protection against that country definitively going Communist. Rather, the situation is reminiscent of Guatemala, where the young people who came suddenly into control of political life after the overthrow of the Ubico dictatorship in 1944, were unable to distinguish between Communists and good national revolutionaries who wanted to bring about land reform, social security, labor legislation, trade unionism, and other long overdue reforms.

The situation is complicated by the fact that most of the Jacobin Left and pro-Communist groups from the remaining dictator countries are now operating out of Cuba. They are able to find there support in terms of finances, men, and political influence, with which they hope to be able to seize control, sooner or later, in their own countries.

The upshot of this may well be that a neutralist régime in Cuba will find friends in Jacobin or pro-Communist governments in the Dominican Republic, Haiti, and Nicaragua. The contagion might well spread to other countries.

The United States' Last Chance

It will perhaps be some time before those last Caribbean dictators are overthrown. The crisis which arose after the overthrow of Batista on January 1, 1959, may even pass, temporarily. However, one thing is certain: no Latin American dictatorship lasts forever. It is only a matter of time until the Trujillo, Duvalier, and Somoza régimes will disappear. Jacobinism, neutralism, and even pro-Communist governments may well supplant them, unless the United States does something about it in the meanwhile.

How much time we have is not clear, but that the United States should radically change its policy on the question of the dictators is very clear. Perhaps the United States may still have time to prove false the claims of the Communists and the neutralists that this country is in principle on the side of the dictators.

The most important, and in many ways the easiest, case is that of Trujillo. This can be done without "intervening" in the Dominican Republic. No one in his right mind, not even the most violent Dominican opponent of Trujillo, would argue in favor of the United States sending troops to oust Trujillo, or even conspiring against him. But the highest officials of the United States government can make clear in public speeches that we believe in democracy in the New World as well as behind the Iron and Bamboo Curtains, that we are as much opposed to the secret police of small Caribbean powers operating in the United States as we are to those of Russia or the satellites doing the same thing. The sympathies of this country for the cause of democracy in the tyrant-ridden countries can be made obvious even without our taking overt steps against their leaders.

The effect of such a change in posture by the United States cannot be overestimated. Undoubtedly one of the things which has weighed most heavily on the opponents of the dictators has been the feeling that the United States is on the side of the tyrants and that it will use its influence to support them. If it were made clear that such is not the case, this would give hope to many of those fighting these régimes. Furthermore, it would go far to convince Latin American democrats that the United States is concerned with tyranny even where such tyranny does not seem to constitute a direct and immediate menace to the national security of this country. Many who might be inclined to be neutralist or even pro-Communist might realize that the best hope for getting democracy in their own countries is to align themselves with the United States in the world-wide struggle for democracy.

A New United States Policy in Inter-American Affairs

Whatever change we make in our attitude toward the Latin American dictators should not be merely one more zigzag in a basically policyless method of dealing with the other American countries. Rather, it should be part of a wider change in outlook, and the result of the adoption of a well defined policy for strengthening inter-American relations. In essence, this policy should be threefold: an abandonment of the attitude of taking Latin America for granted; a general position favoring democracy against dictatorship in the New World; and a program of real economic cooperation for the development of the Latin American nations.

If some casual statements are made about the democracy versus dictatorship problem by high officials of the United States government, and then the matter is dropped until the next crisis appears, little will have been gained. That will not convince either the Latin Americans or those in this country who are concerned with these matters, that the United States government really means what it says.

Rather, it must become the practice of the highest officials of our administration to devote at least a little time and a little discussion in public speeches to the problems of inter-American relations. There are many instances when this is possible. The reception of ambassadors' credentials, for instance, could generally be made the occasion for such statements, and statements made in such instances should be given the widest publicity throughout the hemisphere. Annual messages to Congress are also a chance for enunciating the general principles of the United States' policy in the hemisphere. The innumerable speeches given by top officials could occasionally have some reference to problems of the New World. Press conferences might be used for the same purpose.

The second ingredient of a new policy toward Latin America should be the adoption of the general principle that we favor democracy against dictatorship in Latin America. Were this made quite clear, it would go far toward making military men who are thinking about *coups d'état* against democratic governments have second thoughts. It would thus materially strengthen the position of democratic governments which are under the constant menace of usurpation of power by their military. At the same time, it would give much hope and encouragement to groups which are fighting the remaining dictators.

The third element of a new policy toward Latin America should be a willingness to deal with the problems of economic development of the Latin American countries in an over-all way and to the limit of our own economic ability in the light of other commitments, foreign and domestic. President Juscelino Kubitschek of Brazil made a suggestion for such an over-all approach to the problem in the middle of 1958, and out of this came the so-called Committee of Twenty-one. However, the United States' attitude toward the matter was one of grudging submission to pressure of the Latin Americans rather than one of taking leadership in a "bold, new effort."

It cannot be overemphasized that a fundamental factor in the United States' dealings with the Latin Americans is the question of "how," which is at least as important as "what." That is to say, what the Latin Americans really are looking for from the United States is some inspiring leadership. What the United States needs to offer is an attitude and proposals which will inspire the imagination of the people and the political leaders of the Latin American republics.

This was the secret of Franklin D. Roosevelt's success in the inter-American field. He was able to inspire imagination, confidence, admiration, and loyalty. The people of Latin America, by and large, had faith in him; they felt that he had their best interests at heart and that he was really giving leadership to the hemisphere. Unless a similar feeling can be aroused now by United States leaders, all the specific measures which this country takes as the result of the constant urging of the Latin Americans will have little positive result in stopping the spread of Jacobinism and neutralism.

The Latin Americans have a kind of schizophrenic attitude toward the United States. Though, on the one hand, they are resentful of the size and power of this country and are anxious to assert their own independence from the United States, at the same time they look to the United States for leadership in the hemisphere. But it must be the kind of leadership that can inspire confidence and enthusiasm among the politically conscious people of the area or it cannot be effective.

Insofar as the program of economic cooperation is concerned, a new over-all approach should be taken. Merely to concede the Inter-American Bank, and to be willing finally to talk about price stabilization of the principal Latin American export products is not enough. Even the new half-billion-dollar fund offered by the United States in 1960 is not enough. Rather, there is needed a frank admission by the United States that what has been done so far in the direction of aiding the rapid growth of the Latin American economies has been insufficient, and a new start is needed.

This new start should commence with an invitation by the United States to the Latin American countries to determine the objectives in terms of economic development which they wish to accomplish within the next five to ten years. This should be followed by a suggestion that they then sit down and figure out among themselves to what degree each individual country and all the Latin American nations together can achieve these objectives with their own resources, and to what degree they will need outside financial and technical aid. This balance sheet should then be presented to the United States, and there should be negotiations between this country and the Latin American republics concerning the possibilities of the United States providing this financial and technical help.

The objectives of the Latin American countries should not be stated in terms of some hypothetical increase in the per capita income of the people of the countries. Rather, they should be in terms of removing the bottlenecks which in each of these nations are hampering the process of economic expansion. Brazil, for instance, has been plagued with shortages of power and transport facilities for several decades. Perhaps attention in that country could be centered on removing these difficulties. Each country has some similar kind of obstacle to its economic progress.

The discussions between the United States and the Latin American countries should center not only on loans, technical assistance, and possible grants, but should also involve discussions of stabilization of the demand and prices for their principal exports at reasonably high levels. Ex-President José Figueres has maintained that in the case of Costa Rica, if the country could calculate within a fairly narrow margin of error its income from coffee for a five- to ten-year period, it could save sufficient out of this income to meet all its relatively limited capital needs. This is undoubtedly true of a number of the other nations also.

Conclusion

It is clear that the relations of the United States with Latin America had reached a state of crisis by 1959, because of an overall lack of United States policy in the hemisphere. For the first time, there was a real danger of an important neutralist bloc developing among the Latin American countries and Cuba was already lined up with the Soviet Union in the United Nations and elsewhere. The resentments against United States friendship for dictators and the frustrations arising from inadequate help to the Latin American development effort had generated a degree of hostility toward the United States which had not been equaled since the worst days of Big Stick diplomacy.

Therefore, the need for recasting the whole policy of the United States toward the Latin American countries is urgent. This revision of policy should be in terms such as will inspire confidence and enthusiasm, and will assure the Latin Americans that this country realizes that it has made some serious mistakes and is going to try to provide the kind of democratic leadership which the rest of the hemisphere expects of us. If there is not such an alteration in the Latin American policy of the United States, we can expect to see the deterioration of this country's relations with the rest of the hemisphere continue until Latin America becomes a first-class trouble area for the United States. This is the eleventh hour. We have some time left, and it behooves this country not to waste it.

INDEX

Political parties are indexed under their respective countries.

209